T0318615

Cambridge Elements ☰

Elements in Histories of Emotions and the Senses
edited by
Jan Plamper
University of Limerick

EMOTIONS AND TEMPORALITIES

Margrit Pernau
Max Planck Institute for Human Development, Berlin

CAMBRIDGE
UNIVERSITY PRESS

CAMBRIDGE
UNIVERSITY PRESS

University Printing House, Cambridge CB2 8BS, United Kingdom

One Liberty Plaza, 20th Floor, New York, NY 10006, USA

477 Williamstown Road, Port Melbourne, VIC 3207, Australia

314–321, 3rd Floor, Plot 3, Splendor Forum, Jasola District Centre, New Delhi – 110025, India

103 Penang Road, #05-06/07, Visioncrest Commercial, Singapore 238467

Cambridge University Press is part of the University of Cambridge.

It furthers the University's mission by disseminating knowledge in the pursuit of education, learning, and research at the highest international levels of excellence.

www.cambridge.org
Information on this title: www.cambridge.org/9781108825122
DOI: 10.1017/9781108918701

First published 2021

A catalogue record for this publication is available from the British Library.

ISBN 978-1-108-82512-2 Paperback
ISSN 2632-1068 (online)
ISSN 2632-105X (print)

Emotions and Temporalities

Elements in Histories of Emotions and the Senses

DOI: 10.1017/9781108918701
First published online: September 2021

Margrit Pernau
Max Planck Institute for Human Development, Berlin
Author for correspondence: Margrit Pernau, pernau@mpib-berlin.mpg.de

Abstract: This Element brings together the history of emotions and temporalities, offering a new perspective on both. Time was often imagined as a movement from the past to the future: The past is gone and the future not yet here. Only present-day subjects could establish relations to other times, recovering history as well as imagining and anticipating the future. In a movement paralleling the emphasis on the porous self, constituted by emotions situated not inside but between subjects, *Emotions and Temporalities* argues for a porous present that is open to the intervention of ghosts coming from the past and from the future. What needs investigating is the flow between times as much as the creation of boundaries between them, which first banishes the ghosts and then denies their existence. Emotions are the most important way by which subjects situate and understand themselves in time.

Keywords: history of emotions, temporalities, hauntology, Muslims, South Asia

ISBNs: 9781108825122 (PB), 9781108918701 (OC)
ISSNs: 2632-1068 (online), 2632-105X (print)

Contents

1 Introduction

After a final battle, Boabdil, the king of Granada, had to surrender his city to the conquering Catholic kings in 1492, bringing to an end more than seven centuries of Muslim rule over Andalusia. On his way to exile, pausing on the hills surrounding the city, he looked back one last time on all he had lost – the Alhambra, the gardens, his kingdom, and his place in life – and heaved a deep sigh. His mother, Ayxa, remonstrated with him: "You do well to weep as a woman over what you could not defend as a man." To this day, the place is known as the *Puerto del Último Suspiro del Moro*: the gate of the Moor's last sigh.

I cannot remember a time when I did not know this story. My father told it multiple times, and it seemed to be something that everyone knew about: a floating trope, which would weave its way into our conversations in different countries and contexts. Many threads come together in this small vignette: it is a moment of intense emotions for the king and his mother – of loss, longing, and nostalgia, of anger and shame. It is also a moment in which times become blurred. The story is told from the vantage point of the historical present, from the moment when the king is standing on the hill and looking back. The intensity of the emotions, however, is predicated on the anticipation of the future, which can no longer be avoided, when the Alhambra, still visible now, will have disappeared from sight and become part of an unattainable past. Finally, the narrative of this moment gained a global currency in the nineteenth century, becoming part of the history and the memories of the past Muslims claimed as their own.

If it was as a floating trope that many people first encountered the story, it also had its more stable textual incarnations. The modern narrative of Boabdil (Abu Abdallah Muhammad XII in Arabic) was first told in the West. In 1807, Chateaubriand, the French nobleman and poet, exiled to Spain during the French revolution, wrote a novel, published in 1821, on the fall of Granada, in which he related the above vignette (2006). The topic was taken up again almost immediately by Washington Irving, an American romantic writer, who in 1826 spent several months living in the Alhambra and looking for hidden treasures and folktales related to the rule of the Moors. *The Tales of the Alhambra*, which he published in 1832, gained worldwide fame and was translated into many languages. Irving was interested not only in folklore, but also in the Spanish chronicles of the conquest of Andalusia, which he read and summarized as a fictional account by a Spanish monk in his *Chronicle of the Conquest of Granada* in 1828 (2017a, 2017b). The sigh of the king and the reproach of his mother feature prominently in both books. From there, the story entered the European romantic imagination, Edward Bulwer Lytton leading the way with his novel *Leila or the Siege of Granada* in 1838, with other writers and painters following in his steps.

In this form, we can read the tale as a story of Orientalist imagination, born in the West and adapted by Muslims, and partly this is true. But there is also another side to it. Medieval Arab literature knew a number of poetic genres to express the feelings of exile and the yearning for the lost city. The Muslims banned from Andalusia – before and after 1492 – wrote their stories into these genres (Masarwah & Tarabieh, 2014). The longing for Andalusia in the nineteenth and twentieth centuries was certainly partly mediated by novels and history books from the West, but it also drew on Arab sources, both poetic and historiographic, and on traveler accounts, both medieval and modern (Civantos, 2020; Molina, 2020; Noorani, 1999). Even more than a history of entangled texts and references, this was a history of entangled emotions, which we can no longer clearly separate into their Western and Eastern components. The admiration for the Moors fighting for their kingdom was not limited to Muslims but was also voiced by Western novelists, in spite of their occasional Orientalism. In the fight between the Spanish Catholics and the Andalusian Muslims, their sympathies were more often than not on the Muslim side. The depictions in Western texts, in turn, resonated with Muslims and shaped the way they would later narrate their own stories of Boabdil and Andalusia.

Novelists and their writings, in turn, fed back into nostalgia. This was no homogenous feeling, neither across languages nor within them. It could refer to very different moments in history, which brought forth a plethora of emotions. In the nineteenth century, the empathy for the sighing king tapped into contemporary Muslim feelings of loss. Even more texts, however, dwelt on Andalusia at the height of its political and cultural power, depicting its patronage of the arts and sciences, its economic prosperity, and the beauty of its architecture (Hali, 1997). Here, nostalgia was tinged with pride in what had once been, and with hope that the traits of character, which had brought forth those times, still slumbered in the breasts of Muslims and could be reawakened. Other histories went back even further, to the conquest of the land by the Arabs and Berbers in 711, adding military valor to the civilizational achievements and recovering the masculinity Queen Ayxa had denied her son (Eksell, 2011; Sharar, 1899; Zaidan, 2010). Toward the end of the twentieth century, the Andalusian memories changed once more. What marked novels such as Salman Rushdie's *The Moor's Last Sigh* (1995), but also literary explorations in the Maghreb and in Syria, was the search for a different, a cosmopolitan and tolerant Islam. This would not only counter the present-day fundamentalist homogenizations, but also constitute a model for the future not borrowed from the West (Granara, 2005; Hirschkind, 2020).

The story of Boabdil, thus, is both things at the same time: It is a historical motif, whose movements can be traced over time and whose transformations can be analyzed with precision – be it the colors that nostalgia, shame, or pride take, or the depictions of the temporalities. But it is also a floating trope, contextualized and adapted every time we retell it, sometimes feeding on the texts and sometimes moving at its own rhythm, from conversation to conversation.

1.1 The Aim of *Emotions and Temporalities*

In this Element, I aim to bring together the history of emotions with research on temporalities and global history. This can be broken down into three arguments. First: Studies in emotions and affect have, for a few years already, aimed at overcoming the dichotomy between emotions as a phenomenon taking place inside subjects and the external world in which they move. For this, they emphasized the relations between subjects and between them and the world. Emotions are no longer conceived inside neatly delineated and bounded subjects, but in the in-between. In the process, these studies have developed a number of tools for thinking with and through relations. *Emotions and Temporalities* aims to replicate this movement for the connections between the past, the present, and the future. Instead of looking at the past and the future (only) as a creation or an imagination of the present, I want to focus on their relations. At the center of attention is the way the past, the present, and the future coconstitute each other to a degree of embroiling not only the linear conception of time, but also the possibility of sharp distinctions between times, because the past and the future are not safely gone or yet to come, but haunt the present with their presence.

Second: Emotions and temporalities – that is, the relations between the past, the present, and the future as imagined and experienced by the actors – are closely interwoven. The experience of time and the way subjects situate themselves within time is imbued with, if not defined by, emotions, and vice versa. Exploring the potential of *Stimmung* (mood, atmosphere), I argue that temporalities create a basic emotional undertone that modulates and shapes individual and distinct emotions. This moves beyond the association of progress with hope, to give just one example, and looks at how the temporalities captured in the concept of progress transform the whole plethora of emotions that subjects experience, from patriotism to spousal and parental love, from compassion to disgust and anxiety, from piety to ambition and boredom. It is through these emotions – through feeling progress, doing progress, and becoming a progressive subject – that knowledge about progress is rendered plausible. Obviously, this is not meant to obliterate differences in emotional experiences and to use the concept of atmosphere to reintroduce homogenized ways of feeling – atmospheres need not pervade an entire society (they can, however, do so at specific times), nor do they affect everyone in the same way.

Third: Global history has produced excellent works on the relation between geographical spaces and between micro and macro scales. Its interest in temporalities has so far been less extensive, focusing on the introduction of global time (Ogle, 2015) and the history of clock time (Barak, 2009; Frumer, 2018; Wishnitzer, 2015), rather than on concepts of temporality as the experience and interpretation of relations between the past, the present, and the future. In this Element, I argue that the emotions at the core of temporalities have to be read from a global perspective. They float globally through a number of tropes ("degeneration," "the new man/the new world," etc.), which resonate with subjects living in different contexts without necessarily being the "same" emotions. Thus, they create emotional communities, which might be based on existing social relations and run parallel to existing connections, but could also transcend them.

The focus in this Element is on conceptual reflections. I envision it as a think piece rather than an elaborate piece of historical writing. I draw the core of my empirical material from my own regional expertise on the North Indian Muslims from 1850 to 1950, while also, whenever I feel the need, reaching out for studies from the larger Islamic world and, where required, Europe as well. Literature on emotions, whether linked to temporalities or not, is still scarce for this region. This Element does not aim at satisfying this need; I am in no position to offer new interpretations of Ottoman or Egyptian history or to revise existing ones. If the questions and reflections I raise here resonate with the regional experts, they will take it forward, as I will do in my ongoing empirical studies of North Indian Muslims and their emotions and temporalities.

Still, offering theoretical reflections from the perspective of North Indian Muslims – considered peripheral not only from a Western perspective, but from the majoritarian Indian and from the Arabo-centric Islamic viewpoints as well – remains unusual in academia. Thus far, the only scholars permitted to omit geographical references from their titles and advance arguments beyond the scope of their empirical material are those working on Western and Central Europe. The debates on the need for Europe's provincialization do not seem to have changed much; this Element is an attempt not to rehearse those arguments again, but instead to "just do it."

Embarking from North Indian Muslims, I will follow their global references – be it to the Hindus of the Bengali Renaissance; to their comrades in the struggle for revolution; to Iranian, Ottoman, or Arab intellectuals; to the protagonists of Young Ireland or Young Italy; or to British or German writers on decline and decadence. Not in every case, and perhaps not even in the majority of cases, will it be possible to trace these references exactly. Similar to the story of Boabdil, a trope such as rebirth appears more or less simultaneously in conversations all over the Islamic world and beyond, with people picking up on fleeting mentions in a conversation or a newspaper article rather than in an elaborate book translated into multiple languages. However, even if tropes are floating, they do not indistinctively float in every direction, nor does every trope resonate with every audience.

Beyond the regional focus, I claim my freedom to bring in any texts through which I find it helpful to analyze this material, without aiming to cover all the debates in the three fields comprehensively. That does not mean that I have lost sight of the problems involved in bringing European interpretations and concepts into the discussion. The strategy I suggest in this Element is to try to overcome the traditional division between historians, conceived as active and in sole charge of the analytical framework, and the interpretation of the historical subjects, providing the empirical material and the source concepts, but otherwise ensconced in a past safely divided from the present. If the past and the present are conceived as embroiled to the extent that they are no longer distinguishable, then interventions do not proceed unilaterally from the present toward the past – historical subjects talk back, they bring their own interpretations to the conversation. The theoretical frame, hopefully, will be the result of such a dialogue (more on this theoretical approach in Section 3.1 on hauntology).

1.2 Time and Temporalities

Let us return to the trope of Boabdil's last sigh. The moment the king casts one last gaze upon Granada and sighs brings together times that often are imagined as neatly distinct: The past, in which he ruled his kingdom, and which is still visible in front of him; the future, in which all of this will only be a painful memory, and which will begin as soon as he turns around and follows the path to exile; and the present, in which the past and the future meet with emotional intensity.

Reinhart Koselleck has declared temporalization to be one of the central characteristics of the "saddle period" (2011), the decades that mark the onset of modernity. Like other concepts, the past and the future, as well as the relation between them, now have a history, and the historical subjects are aware of this history (Hölscher, 2016; Koselleck, 2004c, 2011). More recently, François Hartog has developed these insights further, claiming that each present is marked by a different set of relations to the past and the future, which he calls regimes of historicity (2015).[1] However, in his work and in that of Koselleck, the focus on relations does not destabilize the temporal categories as such: The past, the present, and the future remain clearly distinguishable from each other and follow in a given, unsubvertible order. The past can be interpreted, but once it is gone, it cannot be brought back; the future can be imagined, but it is not there yet and will arrive in its own time. In a way, the presentism that Hartog bemoans, the contemporary inability to develop meaningful relations to the past or the future, is already inbuilt into his core assumptions: Only the present can reach out to the past or the future and initiate relations through their interpretations and anticipations – the past and the future are perceived as passive. It is no wonder that the image of temporal layers that Koselleck used to depict the contemporaneity of the past was borrowed from geology. The past may be there, but in most cases it will be hidden and in need of an intervention by present-day archeologists for its excavation (Koselleck & Gadamer, 2000; Hoffmann & Franzel, 2018). Much as this seems natural to us today, historically this was not the only way to think about temporalities, nor need it be the only way we can conceive of time.

The end of the linguistic turn comes with a desire for an experience and a presence that go beyond representation in language, an immediacy that can be felt at the level of the body. A "presence-based relationship to the world" (Gumbrecht, 2004: xv) is as much a spatial as a temporal category. In the field of temporalities, this has given rise to inquiries that focus on the presence of the past – that is, on relations that no longer emanate from the present and lead to a social construction of the past, but in which agency rests with the past itself. These attempts moved in different directions. Koselleck, rather tentatively, explored experiences that "pour into one's body like fiery lava and congeal there" (2020: 2), remaining present as a frozen block of the past that can neither be wholly translated into language and communicated to other people, nor reimagined and changed by the present. Trauma studies focus on how the past continues to act on the present (Leys, 2000), forcing people to constantly relive

---

[1] I prefer "temporalities" to "regimes of historicity," in order to avoid the misunderstanding that the past is at the center of the current investigation. I use the plural to underline the multiple temporalities at work at the same time, and I forgo the use of "regimes," as a number of the temporalities I will focus on were developed from the margins of the state, rather than by groups in power.

scenes from the past. Psychoanalytical reflections, in turn, show how the past moves the present and intrudes into history writing (Runia, 2014).

Moving back from psychology to history, Achim Landwehr has suggested the category of chronoference as a way of referencing the creation of relations between times that are absent and those that are present. The flow of relations moves in both directions, thus undermining the dualism (and the well-defined boundaries) between the present and the past and the present and the future, and creating what he calls the "absent presence of the past." This brings together the traditional absence of the past – once past, it can never return – and its ongoing presence. The focus, Landwehr elaborates, can thus be neither on the past nor the present, but only on their relation (2016: 149–65).

These studies have opened up our conceptions about possible relations between times to an extent that the temporalities of North Indian Muslims can now be brought into the picture. Former disciplinary belief in the naturalness of the boundaries between the past, the present, and the future, and in their linear sequence, risked making any alternative imaginations look quaint or Oriental at best, or point to a failure to understand properly the flow of history at worst. Here, the recent focus on relationality between times (less of a new idea in philosophy and anthropology than for empirical history writing), which might be initiated from the present, but also from the past or the future, creates a meeting ground.

At least until the middle of the nineteenth century, the ubiquitous presence of the past was a common experience for the Muslims of North India. Not only were Sufi saints known for their longevity – at times extending to several hundred years, allowing them to bridge epochs – even their death did not put an end to their presence and their possibilities of interacting with their devotees in the present. Thus, the character of a city space was marked not only by the living, but also by the presence of those, holy or less so, who had lived there earlier (Pernau, 2019b). What held true of people also applied to poetry and other works of art: They were not regarded as documents of the past, but shared time with the present. These perceptions were embedded in religious time, in the trajectory from the eternity before creation (*azal*) to the eternity after the Day of Judgment (*abad*). Even more important is the copresence of eternity and secular time, as manifested in the revelation and in the person of the Prophet Muhammad, whose existence as the divine light preceded the creation of the world, and who still graces certain gatherings with his presence, but also in the many wonders, great and small, through which God intervenes in the world (Faruqi, 1995).

Taken together, what this allows us to do is to flip the question of temporal relations: Most Western tradition has long thought of times as neatly, even naturally, separated from each other. Work was needed to create relations between previously unrelated entities. What if it were the other way round? What if the present, the past, and the future already existed in synchronicity, and the work of modern subjects was directed to establishing their difference and guarding the boundaries between them, preventing the past and the future from spilling over into the present? What if it was not asynchronicity that was the given, the natural state to be overcome by synchronization (Jordheim, 2017), but the overcoming of a synchronicity, which could no longer be accommodated in linear thinking? These reflections constitute the core of *Emotions and Temporalities*.

1.3 Global Emotions, Global Temporalities

From its beginning as a self-described field in the 1980s, the history of emotions, and even more so the anthropology of emotions, had a strong tendency toward studies that were locally bounded, whether the locality was as small as a village or a tribe or as large as a modern nation. At the time, this seemed the only way to counteract the universalizing claims of experimental psychology, to emphasize the historicity of emotions, and to embed them in culture (amongst others, see Abu Lughod, 1986; Lutz, 1988). This came at a price: The local had to be stripped of its connections to the outside world and became incommensurable. The history of encounters and relations largely fell outside the purview of these studies; if it was brought in at all, it was not given much of an explanatory status.

This changed with the rise of transnational and global history, bringing to the fore a focus on the movement of people and of texts. The trajectory of the history of Boabdil's sigh, moving between Granada, France, the United States, the Arab World, India, and back, shows that following emotions beyond the local need not mean subscribing to a universal take on emotions. The anticipated nostalgia of the king, to which so many could relate over the centuries, was not a basic emotion or one that is wired in the brain, but a historically and culturally specific emotion, which could and did change its meaning over time and space.

Global exchanges intensified the flow of temporal tropes and the emotions linked to them. Travels brought about a face-to-face encounter with unfamiliar emotions, which found their reflection in travelogues, an increasingly popular genre in the Islamic world since the nineteenth century (Gammerl, et al., 2019; Majchrowicz, 2015). Travels, moreover, went hand in hand with increased access to written sources: Libraries, publishing houses, and the offices of journals were frequent stopovers for travelers, who brought home not only books, but also the knowledge of how to access them in the future. From the 1860s onwards, recent English publications, novels, and volumes of poetry, as well as scholarly treatises, increasingly found their way to North Indian libraries and private collections (Joshi, 2002; Pernau, 2019a: 179–86); the same held true for books, journals, and newspapers in Persian and Arabic, and to some extent even in Ottoman Turkish.

Intense and scholarly engagement with these texts, in the original or through translation, however, was not the only, and perhaps even not the most important, way tropes and emotions wandered and created global connections. Most ideas reached readers not through entire books, but through conversations, through summaries and digests in journals, or through even briefer references, evoking rather than elaborating a concept, an image, or a narrative. This very brevity, which left much to the imagination of the reader or listener, did not hinder but, on the contrary, facilitated the re-embedding of these allusions into a familiar context. Not much detailed knowledge was needed to feel pride in the rule of the Abbasids or the kings of Andalusia, in their civilizational achievements at a time when Europe was still mired in darkness; to experience a sense of brotherhood with the fighters for Young Italy or Young Ireland; to weep for those who sacrificed their lives fighting for their country's freedom.

I suggest the concept of resonance to capture these transmissions of emotions.[2] Resonance reproduces and amplifies the vibration of one subject in another. Unlike an echo, it is based on a previous similarity between the subjects. The recognition and acknowledgment of resonance is a strong emotional experience, an experience of community, not through sharing abstract values, but through recognizing one's own feelings and desires in another person, and vice versa. Resonance involves a sensory and affective experience (Böhme 2017: 167–68; Eisenlohr, 2018).

The fluid feeling communities based on resonance could transcend the limits of empires and nations.[3] They were not exclusive, but allowed for multiple overlaps. Nevertheless, they were not situated outside the world of power. Encounters, even at this fleeting level, needed material bases. Travelers relied on established routes and on means of transport. Though manuscript texts, too, had circulated widely, the commercialization of print allowed circulation to an extent never previously imagined. Even more importantly, if resonance was based on a previous similarity, this similarity, in turn, was premised on the

---

[2] For a different use of the concept, focusing on the creations of relations to the world, see Rosa, 2019.

[3] The concept of fluidity was developed in conversation with gender studies and queer theory (for detailed references, see Davis, 2009; Barua, et al., forthcoming [2021]), rather than referring to Zymunt Baumann's *Liquid Modernity* (2000).

shared experiences of the age of European colonialism, decolonization, and global capitalism. Communities needed common experiences, as well as interpretations of these experiences as shared and as emotionally resonating in their members' own souls.

1.4 Emotions and *Stimmung*

Let us return to Boabdil one last time. Nostalgia, based on the sense of imminent or actual loss, is a strong emotion, and one that resonated with many colonial subjects and their experiences of loss. The moor's last sigh implicated more than that: His mother's cruel taunt, which not only held him responsible for the loss, but also imputed this to a deficiency in his masculinity, is an integral part of the narrative. Rather than only nostalgia, what Boabdil's story shows is a pain shot through with shame, or at least with the effort to induce shame, and, through shame, the desire to not only moan, but to recover an active and honorable role in the world.

Emotions are central to the experience of time, and hence to the analysis of temporal relations. Hardly any text evoking a glorious past, calling for a reawakening and rejuvenation, or sounding the clarion call for revolution fails to mention emotions: hope, despair, pride, honor, and shame most central among them. On one level, this can be explained by the motivational power of emotions: Most of these texts were not abstract philosophical reflections on times and their changes, but wanted to contribute to changing the world. Take Altaf Husain Hali, who exclaimed in *The Ebb and Flow of Islam* that he had only written the poem "in order to make my friends and fellows feel a sense of outrage [*ghairat*] and shame [*sharam*]" (1997: 97). Or take the revolutionary Har Dayal, who exhorted young people: "Mankind anxiously asks if there is a way out of the gloom and horror of to-day into light and life. It is for you to blaze the trail for great movements that will build up a happier world" (1934: 1). The sources themselves guide us to these feelings; our task, as always, is to properly historicize the emotions, and to explore the precise meanings of outrage and shame, or gloom, horror, and happiness, and how they felt for the historical subjects in that precise place and time before using them as an explanation.

Emotions, however, do more than mobilize people to recover the past or to conquer the future. On another level, they create knowledge about time and temporalities, and endow knowledge created through other means with plausibility. Plausibility is usually associated with intellectual investigations, focusing on the coherence of the argument, on its relation to what subjects already know, on the way newly introduced elements support or contradict the familiar narratives. The emotions to which this knowledge gives rise are hardly less important. It is the affective resonance of knowledge, the way it makes subjects feel and contributes to their sense of identity, that is crucial for the acceptance of ways of thinking about the past, the present, and the future. To give just one example: For readers in India, the Ottoman Empire, or Egypt, reading Darwin or Spencer and agreeing with their interpretation of the natural or social world and its evolution was much more than learning something new, the acceptance or rejection of which would be based on the persuasiveness of the arguments. Rather, it implied becoming a certain kind of person and owing allegiance to specific groups and not others (Elshakry, 2013). The emotional resonance the texts evoked was decisive in tilting the balance one way or the other. The very weight held by arguments framed as scientific depended on the emotional valence and resonance of science.

From this, it will already have become clear that I am interested in more than carefully delimited single emotions, as if we could talk about hope without also taking into consideration anxiety and shame and love and many others. Looking for what holds them together, discussions on *Stimmung* have been particularly helpful. Unlike mood, *Stimmung* covers the subjective and the objective side of emotions at the same time: A space can have a *Stimmung*, an atmosphere into which subjects can enter and which may transform the way they are feeling. It also refers to the subjective side of feelings: A person can be in a specific *Stimmung*: for instance, an angry or a hopeful mood (Böhme, 2017; Gumbrecht, 2004). Etymologically, *Stimmung* references the tuning of an instrument, from which it retains its affective and sensory connotation (Wellbery, 2010). It is particularly apt for describing the relational and interactive quality of emotions, their tuning in with the surroundings and with other emotions present in the same space. Urdu poetry would use *rang o bu*, the "color and fragrance" of a situation, or talk about *ab o hawa*, the "water and air" of a place, which also stand in for its climate. If these expressions might translate as atmosphere rather than mood, it is an atmosphere that pervades the porous boundaries of the subjects, floats through them like a perfume, and colors the world in which they live and all the emotions they feel.[4]

The organization of *Emotions and Temporalities* proceeds along a number of tropes, familiar to the historical subjects, which explore the presence of the past and the future in the present; deciding whether a particular trope belongs to the past or the future was more difficult than I had anticipated. These concepts, I argue, not only provide the foundation for the interpretation of the subjects'

---

[4] I would like to thank my Facebook community, who discussed the proper translation of "atmosphere" and "mood" with me, and especially my dear friend Carla Petievich, from whom, once again, I learned so much.

place in time and the possibilities and imperatives that this entailed for their acting in the world, but also carry an emotional valence, which allowed for their resonance. To a certain extent, the selection of the tropes is subjective: They are the concepts that come up most regularly in the sources and secondary works I have read. In theory, it might be possible to back up this selection with a multilingual digital-humanities project, investigating newspapers and journals and quantifying the results, but I am not sure the additional precision would warrant the investment.

2 The Presence of the Past

2.1 Ghosts and Jinns

In *A Secular Age*, the philosopher Charles Taylor introduces the distinction between a porous and a buffered self. The porous self, which he identifies with the enchanted world of the premodern, can be permeated by the outside world, by spirits, by the emotions and the thoughts of other people, whereas the buffered self, a phenomenon belonging to the secular age, has stable boundaries and thus controls what can enter it. This does not prevent the establishment of relations, either to other selves or to the world, but the core of self is no longer situated in a relational in-between, but on the inside (2007: 35–41). In this context, I am less interested in the dichotomy between the premodern and the modern and its link to the analytical categories of the enchanted and the secular than in the implications of clogging the pores, establishing boundaries, and thus creating – real or imaginary – autonomous selves who own their emotions. I find this an image useful to think about both emotions and temporalities and the relations between them.

The concept of the porous self resonates with the classical Indo-Persian ways of thinking about the self and its emotions. Drawing on Aristotelian concepts, texts on morality (*akhlaq*) depict the ideal virtuous self as needing to avoid excess and to keep the emotions in a state of balance. This emotion management, however, can never be limited to the individual's own feelings, but extends to the feelings that a person encounters, as emotions do not belong to one individual, but float between multiple ones: The self is its relations. The buffered self, on the other hand, has a core that is independent of relations and exists before them – logically and often temporally as well. Instead of striving for harmony with its surroundings, the buffered self develops boundaries and an internal consistency, which transcend its changing surroundings: "To thy own self be true." This enhances the buffered self's sense of authenticity and autonomy, but also of disconnectedness (Pernau, 2019a).

The transformation of the self and its emotions, I would like to suggest, is replicated at the level of temporalities. The porous present is distinguished from the past, but its boundaries remain permeable. The past may exist on a different plane than the present, but it is not gone and remains linked to the present in multiple ways. The buffered present aims at closing these boundaries and at preventing the past (and the future) from flowing in and out. It is now only through the discipline of history that the past can be accessed; the agency for this rests with the present only. Like the self, the present has started being imagined as autonomous, delegitimizing and even denying the possibility of any other way of relating to the past. Nineteenth-century claims that the Orient lacked a proper history, therefore, are as much about a lack of the newly hegemonic access to the past (i.e., of history writing) as about an excess of other approaches to it.

The investigations by historians since the 1970s of the ways the past has been created, nations and their histories imagined, and traditions invented have discarded the notion of a stable past, waiting to be discovered and then narrated the way it actually was. By showing the implication of historians in the creation of the past, these investigations have, however, fortified the boundaries of the present – any relation to other times can only be initiated by the present, which is the only time purportedly endowed with agency. We can relate to the past, but *we* have to take the initiative; imagining an active role for the past itself is no longer admissible in academic contexts (or was not until quite recently, at least among historians). This, however, does not mean a return to a Rankean concept of the past: The past for which I am claiming an active role lacks the solidity with which Ranke endowed it, remaining fluid, ghostlike, and plural.

Unlike what its embedding in a narrative of secularization and modernization suggests, this transition from porous selves and times to buffered ones is neither ever complete nor irreversible. Even before affect studies refocused our atten-tion on the in-betweenness of feelings, psychoanalysis had already undermined the belief that the past was gone and no longer impinged on the present; studies on trauma and on memory reinforced these tendencies, most recently joined by theories of materiality emphasizing the agency of objects, past and present. The much-needed emphasis that the linguistic turn had placed on the importance of language and other sign systems in shaping humans' interpretation of the world has given way to a different register in the last decade or two. The stress affect studies places on the nonrepresentational, on intensity not yet mediated by culture, is mirrored in the quest for a presence of the past that is more real than a representation or a construction. Both are often couched in a language foregrounding the "desire for immediacy" (Gumbrecht, 2004: xiv), for authen-ticity and visceral experiences, favoring an access to the world through the body and the senses rather than through concepts (39). Furthermore, neither are premised on specific emotions or affects, but partake of the same atmosphere, the same way of relating to the world, bodily and emotionally. In itself, this longing for a relation to the past that is not mediated by representation provides no indication of the possibility of its fulfillment: Historians and philosophers of history can well yearn for what might be irretrievably lost. Still, it makes it worthwhile exploring what we might gain by a dialogue with other presents that were more porous and more open to perceiving different presences than our own time.

One of the central images Reinhart Koselleck uses in his theory of history to depict the pluralities of the past and their relation to the present is the geological process of sedimentation, leading to layers of time (*Zeitschichten*) piled on top of each other. Beneath each present, he claims, there exists a multitude of pasts that have not vanished, but remain copresent with our own times (Koselleck & Gadamer, 2000; also Hoffmann & Franzel, 2018; Jordheim, 2011; Lorenz, forthcoming [2021]). This brings a welcome complexity to questions of periodization and of diachronic change. The metaphor leaves open, however, how the presence of the past actually works: Is it simply there, passively and without agency? Is it a resource that present subjects can draw upon and reactivate, thereby underlining the exclusive agency of the present? Answers to these questions might differ according to the area under investigation; access to older layers being easier for the history of concepts – where it might just be a matter of ordering an old book from the stacks and reintroducing it into the debate – than for that of social structures (Langewiesche, 2021). What all these approaches have in common is that the past, even if present, is set in stone. Except as a volcanic eruption (which Koselleck does not mention in this context), it does not interact with the present nor challenge its boundaries.

A radically different way of conceiving the presence of the past is through the ghost – a fluid figure if ever there was one. Ghosts, long abhorred as a symbol of superstition, have gained academic respectability through Derrida's concept of hauntology. Like a ghost, the past emerges into the present; Hamlet's ghost, its quest for justice denied in the past, and the challenge it poses to the present, constitute Derrida's literary starting point (2006: 1). The past in the form of a ghost is no longer set in stone and waiting for the historian, but can come in different shapes, flowing through the boundaries with which the buffered self and the buffered present have tried to protect themselves.

However, ghosts, too, need to be provincialized, as they link the past and the present in a multitude of different ways. Also, not all spirits evoke the same feelings, and certainly not all of them are terrifying. These presences can be spirits of humans who have died and who still haunt their former spaces – as is the case of Hamlet's ghost. More important for the everyday life – not only in the premodern time, but also today – is the interaction with saints (usually classified as spirits rather than ghosts), who, though dead, still retain the possibility of communicating with their disciples from within their graves over the centuries, answering to their requests, and guiding and protecting them (Pernau, 2019b). The Prophet himself is believed to be present at certain rituals, most notably during the Milad ceremony, celebrating his birthday, besides interacting with believers in their dreams (Felek & Knysh, 2012; Mittermaier, 2011). In these cases, the Prophet both is and is not a historical figure: He is at the same time the human being who lived and fought in Arabia in the seventh century, and the light preceding the creation of the world, copresent in every present. Though overwhelming, the interaction with him would not be marked by fear, but by awe, respect, and love.

Jinns, whom God created from fire, are different from the presences that once were living human beings, created from earth. Though their lifespan extends to hundreds of years, they are born, procreate, and die, and constitute an inter-mediate category between humans and angels. Jinns are shape-shifters, often taking the body of an animal, and while some of them are evil and frightening, others are not. Especially in South Asia, the line between jinns and saints is somewhat blurry, and jinns are also addressed with requests for help, by both Hindus and Muslims. Jinns are a familiar presence, not as awe inspiring as the major Sufi saints, but then they also can never be trusted completely. Their longevity establishes a link between different times; some of the oldest jinns were already alive at the time of the Prophet, thus blurring the hierarchical vision of history, premised on the classification of generations according to their proximity to the Prophet. If jinns were companions of the Prophet, those who communicated with them were only one generation removed from him, with all that this implies for their status.[5]

While the interpretation of jinns and the practices through which people related to them were (and are) strongly localized, the debates on these forms of presence among Muslim reformers since the beginning of the nineteenth century drew on exchanges among scholars from different regions of the Islamic world (Pernau & Stille, 2021). The Quran mentions jinns at several instances, which made it difficult, if not impossible, for the reformers to discard them simply as superstition. Instead, they chose a symbolic interpretation, taking the jinns to stand for people with a fiery temperament (Khan, 1962), or

---

[5] Taneja, 2018, and personal communication, October 6, 2020. For investigations on jinns, mainly focusing on the Arab world, see Nünlist, 2015; El-Zain, 2009.

read them as an anticipation of medical research and a reference to microbes and germs.

From the Enlightenment onward, the fight against the belief in ghosts, spirits, jinns, and other forces perforating the boundaries of the self and the present has been presented as a liberation from fear: Goya's painting of the sleep of reason producing monsters. Reformers in Europe and in the Muslim world saw their discarding of ghosts as a step toward the creation of free and autonomous personalities, confident and able to take responsibility for the world they created. As noted, however, the emotions involved in these encounters are more equivocal than it seems at first sight. Ghosts, jinns, and spirits may be experienced as disturbing and terrifying, but not all of them are the same, and beliefs and experiences vary extensively from region to region. Even if they are frightening, it does not mean that humans are completely at their mercy – there are time-honored strategies to deal and negotiate with them, as well as to profit from them. The presence of saints, and above all the Prophet, evokes awe rather than terror, but also trust, devotion, and love – emotions that in turn need to be investigated in more detail. We have by now excellent studies on the transformations of conjugal and romantic love, but the history of the love for the Prophet remains to be written.

Historians have few problems with ghosts and jinns as long as they remain safely confined to an actors' category. Some of them are even willing to take the belief in ghosts seriously. The historian's task, they explain, is not to judge the belief, but to observe its effects – a position that, in spite of its purported agnosticism, posits that what is effective is the belief in the ghost, not the ghost itself (Chakrabarty, 2001: 16, 104–6; Clossey, et al., 2016). This, however, is not agnosticism, but a firm claim that ghosts do not exist and hence cannot act, and they certainly cannot link present and absent times.

What I suggest here is to go a step further. If we forgo the decision on whether ghosts are real, if, in Ethan Kleinberg's elegant formulation, the past (with its ghosts) is present (2017), crossing out the word endows the quality of being with ambivalence: It is and is not at the same time, but even where it is not, the traces of being remain visible. This might allow us to imagine temporality differently. We have learned to take the bufferedness of the present for the natural and only possible order of things. In the unidirectional sequence of the past, the present, and the future, relations to other times can only be initiated by the present. History writing is the only legitimate way of connecting with the past – history becomes a discipline. It is this discipline, above all, which can be trusted, far more than memory or trauma.

If instead we were to start with the presence of ghosts and jinns from the past, what is happening since the nineteenth century can be seen as an exorcism, an attempt to ban the spirits and establish boundaries they are no longer supposed to cross. However, not all exorcisms are successful, and lately, since the end of the linguistic turn's hegemony, historians have struggled to find ways to talk about the continued presence of the past (Ghosh & Kleinberg, 2013; Huyssen, 2003; Landwehr, 2016; Lorenz, et al., 2013). I believe ghosts help us in this task. They are more fluid and active than Koselleck's rock formations, and unlike traumata, they are everyday phenomena. They are material, but not quite, and above all, they allow us to enter into a dialogue with the historical actors – both those who believed in spirits and their agency and those who wanted to exorcise them.

This suggestion is linked to the debate of provincializing our analytical categories (Chakrabarty, 2001) and takes it a step further. European concepts, historically developed to interpret and bestow meaning on the experiences of European subjects, stand in a line of continuity with the concepts we use today in the social sciences and in history writing – here, too, the past has an uncanny presence. Once these same concepts are used for the analysis of experiences that differ regionally, culturally, or even socially, this leads to dislocations. Concepts from non-European languages (increasingly, from any language other than English) can only enter the academic discussion once they have been translated and either made comparable or turned into the description of a lack: Dharma or Confucianism is religion, the North Indian *ashraf* are a middle class, but not quite. The history of concepts, I have suggested elsewhere, might not only help to identify this problem, but also point toward a solution through the integration of different conceptual histories into the analytical categories (Pernau, 2013, 2016).

The investigation of ghosts and jinns has shown that it is not only concepts that are not admissible in academia in their vernacular shape and require translation, but also certain beliefs, interpretations, and ways of being in the world and in time. While the secular liberal or Marxist can hold the same set of beliefs – in values but also in causalities – inside and outside of academia, irrespective of the Christian heritage of their teleology, beliefs in ghosts or even in God are required to be kept outside or translated out of recognition. There are certainly good reasons that may be advanced to keep it that way, but we also need to address the processes of exclusion that this involves. If it is only European experiences (some, not all) and interpretations which feed into our analytical categories, what would happen if we try to reverse these exclusions and base our interpretation on the historical actors' experiences of ghosts and jinns (some, not all)? For this Element, the question of the modalities of the ghosts' existence might be the least interesting aspect, and can be kept at bay. To those who fear that using ghosts as a category of analysis might blur the distinction between analytical and historical concepts, it might be suggested that if the discussion on provincialization has taught us anything, then it would be the fact that these categories have always been blurred to a much greater extent that we usually care to admit. Without challenging the epistemological foundation of historiography, it might be useful to experiment with ways of writing that overcome the distinction between beliefs and concepts that can directly enter the narrative because they are a pre-history of "our" beliefs and concepts, and those that have to be sanitized and translated before gaining admission. A dialogue, however, does not mean that the historian has to renounce her own concepts. This Element is not a history of ghosts in the Islamic world; rather, ghosts work here as an analytical category, which is developed in dialogue with the sources provided by the historical actors, but not identical to any of their multiple concepts.

On the positive side, it is the very indeterminacy of the concept of ghosts that directs our attention to phenomena that might evade more clear-cut categories. Ghosts do not allow us to represent the nonrepresentational, but at least they alert us to its continuous presence. In the following analysis, the reversion to traditional modernist tropes might seem at first sight like a disappointing giving up on the theoretical potential of hauntology. However, thinking with and through ghosts allows us to reflect on porosity and fluidity, on efforts to live with them, but also on efforts to clog the pores, erect stable boundaries, and exorcize the ghosts inherent in these very concepts.

2.2 Stages of Development

In an oft-quoted article, Reinhart Koselleck has shown how around the time of the French Revolution, the space of experience and the horizon of expectation parted company. For the subjects of the age of revolutions, the present was so new and so different from everything they had known before, they concluded that the past no longer provided guidance to the future, and history was no longer the teacher of life (2004b, 2004c). To the excitement and the adventure of discovering and exploring unknown parts of the globe (unknown to Europeans, that is), corresponded the feeling of standing on the brink of a new time, with risks, certainly, but also with unexplored possibilities, waiting to be conquered. This reference to the emotions involved evidently needs much fine-tuning. The feelings of venturing into an unexplored future were not the same at the end of the eighteenth century as at the end of the nineteenth; Germany felt it had more catching up to do than England; the middle classes were more engaged with the future than others; and, finally, for a long time, this was a male project. Still, it created an atmosphere of expectancy, of possibility, which pervaded most spheres of life.

This feeling was both underwritten and undermined by the model of historical stages of development prominently put forth by Scottish philosophers of the Enlightenment, but also widely debated in Germany and France. Every society, they claimed, went through stages leading from the savagery of the early cave dwellers, through barbarity, to the present age of commerce and civility, embodied to perfection by contemporary Britain and, to a slightly lesser degree, by some continental European countries. For them, the model did indeed offer a vision of an open future, and no experience could tell where it would lead them – though they drew on a strong belief from the past in the perfectibility of humans and in the progress of their societies. For all the others, the future was not unknown, but had already happened elsewhere. The very universality of the timeline meant that all societies would follow the same trajectory, though they might enter history at different times and proceed at different speeds. If they were still moored at an earlier stage, the history of Britain or Europe (and a little later, America) showed them what the future had in stock for them. For the vast majority of people, especially those living in the colonies, there were still lessons to be learned from history – if not from their own, then at least from those ahead of them. Their conquest of the future was less a venture into the unknown and more of a struggle to catch up and to hurry along a path already traced by others. It was marked less by a self-confident heroism and more by the sense that something went wrong; by worry, anxiety, and even shame.

The stages of development were distinguished by their economic conditions. Hunters and gatherers made way for shepherds and finally for settled agriculture; technology facilitated commerce and, in the end, industrialization. They were also set apart by their legal regimes. If despotism was a sign of the Middle Ages (and its Oriental incarnations), the present and future were marked by fair and equal law. Civilized individuals increasingly participated in self-government, with civil society providing a powerful check on the state. The most important indicators to distinguish between different stages, however, were the character and manners of their inhabitants, their habitual emotions, and the practices to which these gave rise. Their civilizational stage became apparent through the way men treated their wives, whether as objects of sensual gratification, jealously controlled at all times, or with tender love and respect; by the courage they displayed in withstanding tyranny or by their cowardly and cringing submission; and by their following of a gentle and rational religion or their fanatical belief in superstitions. Only a buffered self, to revert to Charles Taylor's concept, would be recognized as truly civilized. These were the people who withstood outside influence, be it of men or ghosts, and who needed no external discipline. They were the masters of their emotions, and their emotions were their own, rather than being feelings of doubtful origin floating through them. Emotions, both ascribed and felt, were thus at the core of the global hierarchy created through the organization of temporalities performed by the trope of the stages of development. Civilized people were strong enough to fight off ghosts, but it was a constant fight, exacerbated by the fact that it could no longer be conceived as a fight against the ghosts themselves, but only against the belief in them.

The model of the stages of development organized history, providing a strong link between temporalities, emotions, and the self. It mapped out spatial differences along a universal timeline, and thereby created a new and hierarchical global order, classifying each society according to its stage in history. These categorizations, in turn, provided the criteria for whether a country would be recognized as a state entitled to the protection of international public law, and which (if any) political rights it might claim from the colonial power. Societies moved along this timeline, poised between the "no more" of the past and the "not yet" of the future.

For all the emphasis Koselleck placed on experience and expectation parting company, the linear model of history was never the only one he was interested in exploring. Linear history, he insisted, is always embedded in structures of repetition, foremost in the cycles of natural time, the recurrence of days and nights, of the seasons, but also of human life and generations. At a deeper level, no representation, but also no organization of social life is possible without the assumption of certain forms of repetition. An event that is completely unique and shows no resemblance to anything known before cannot be named (though it may have a presence). Nor is meaningful action possible if its results cannot be anticipated. Without these assumptions, "humanity would plunge into a bottomless void" (Koselleck, 2000: 15, my translation; see also Koselleck, 2018; Simon, 2019) – a remarkable image, capturing the relation between the concepts ordering temporalities and the depth of the nonrepresentational, which, like ghosts, can be alluring and desired, but also terrifying.

At one level, the fact that the model of the stages of development became widely accepted in the Indo-Islamic world (as in the rest of the world) was the result of colonial power dynamics. If the classification of a society along the developmental timeline had a crucial impact on its global ranking, it made more sense to challenge one's place on this timeline or to attempt to move ahead by taking over the agenda of the civilizing and self-civilizing mission than to oppose the model as a whole. For instance, Saiyid Ahmad Khan (1817–98), reformer, educationist, and loyalist to the British, acknowledged the diagnosis that Indian Muslims lacked civilization in comparison with the European powers (but were far ahead compared to Africans, and even Afghans). It was up to his coreligionists, he explained, to shed their superstitions, not least their belief in jinns, and acquire the knowledge and character to move ahead along the civilizational path (Pernau, 2019b).

At another level, the Enlightenment philosophy of history did not sound as unfamiliar to an Indo-Islamic audience as the colonial powers would have wanted to imagine, especially if we do not reduce it to its linear variations. The interpretation of history by Enlightenment philosophers was never homogeneous. At roughly the same time that Scottish philosophers propagated unidirectional progress, Rousseau saw history as a long decline from the stage of nature, whereas Montesquieu held onto a modified version of cyclical history – not to forget Gibbon's *History of the Decline and Fall of the Roman Empire*, which remained influential throughout the nineteenth century. In an Islamicate context, these models resonated with familiar ways of conceptualizing changing times; this contributed to making them plausible to their new audience. Already in the fourteenth century, Ibn Khaldun, the Arab polymath, had developed a cyclical view of societies, observing the alterations between a sedentary civilization, its weakening and defeat at the hand of nomadic Berbers, who drew their force from tribal forms of solidarity before settling down after their victory and becoming sedentary and civilized in turn. This cycle, he argued, took about three generations to complete and start anew (1958). Ibn Khaldun had provided arguments for political debates in the Ottoman Empire since the late sixteenth century (Sariyannis, 2019: 279–325). In India, he was known in scholarly circles at least since the eighteenth century, probably not through the Arabic original, but mediated by the Ottoman scholar Katip Çelebi (d.1657) (Ernst, 2016). Nearer home, Shah Wali Ullah (1703–62), an Islamic scholar and reformer from Delhi, claimed as spiritual ancestor by most Indian Muslim reformist movements of the nineteenth and twentieth centuries, predated the Scottish models by a generation in explaining the changes in history through four stages of development. His model, though linear in principle, allowed for a decline and reversion to earlier stages if the rulers did not live up to their duties. This allowed him to turn his model into a tool explaining what he saw as the corruption of the Mughal Empire. Instead of ruling in accordance with the norms of the sharia, patronizing religious scholars, and defending their realm, he saw the rulers and the court as seeking only their own personal pleasures and diverting their patronage to musicians and courtesans. As they refused his appeal to reform their personal lives, he called for the transfer of power into more able hands, embodying a sterner piety and martial virtues (Hermansen, 2005: 113–41; Syros, 2012).

The desire for clear boundaries and their partial establishment became important in a number of ways. The disentanglement of Hindu and Muslim practices, for instance, has received much academic attention. The classification of the stages of the past limited these periods, and hence also the past itself, to well demarcated spaces. The stages did not follow each other with the certainty of scientific rules, but the agency to subvert them belonged either to God or to a human actor living in the present. To this corresponds the attempt of Shah Wali Ullah and the reformers following his program to curtail the intercessory practices at the shrines and the mediatory role of the Sufi saints, aimed less, however, at human autonomy than at a restoration of divine sovereignty. While the role of the Prophet as a model for everyday behavior grew in importance, practices centered on the affective experience of his presence – like the celebrations of his birthday, the *milad un nabi*, each of which he was believed to grace with his own presence – increasingly came under critique (Tareen, 2019). Even after the belief in jinns had lost ground, God, the Prophet, and their temporality could interrupt the order of secular time at any given moment.

Once these historical models were translated into political arguments, the difference between linear and cyclical history was no longer a categorical one, but a matter of degree. As we have seen, linear histories only in rare instances excluded structures of repetition and the possibility to link the present back to the experience of the past – the decline of the Roman Empire was read as a warning against the dangers of excessive civilization, even at the heyday of British belief in progress. In the colonial context, decline was a necessary figure of thought to explain how India and China could be seen as lacking in civilization, in spite of the fact that artifacts pointed to the presence of refined cultures at a time when Europe was still enveloped in the darkness of the early Middle Ages. On the other hand, cyclical theories hardly ever discounted some possibility of human agency to avert or at least postpone decline, through piety or virtue or a combination of both. The stages of development were thus an attempt to buffer the present and to make it similar to the new sense of self, but the old ghosts continued to loom only just out of sight.

2.3 The Golden Age

The trope of the Golden Age has a long history. Greek antiquity, notably in the works of Hesiod, knew of a period when humans lived in a world of abundance, peace, and happiness, without suffering from illnesses or old age. This period was followed by decline, the Golden Age turning into silver, then into bronze, and finally into iron. This trope was taken up in the Old Testament, where the Book of Daniel describes periods of successive decline also using metallurgic metaphors. Hindu cosmology describes four ages, starting from the *satyayuga*, the age of truth, to the present *kaliyuga*, the age of decline and disruption, which ends in chaos before the cycle starts all over again (González-Reimann, 2016; Sarkar, 1998). In the Islamic world, visions of the Golden Age – be it the commonwealth at Medina or a period when society had excelled in virtue – for a long time formed part of advice literature, providing orientation and warning of the dangers of present decline (Sariyannis, 2019: 188–232).

The second half of the nineteenth century saw the proliferation of the trope of the Golden Age. If the stages of development were based on a universal timeline for all societies, thus holding up hope even for those still lagging behind, Darwin's research had extended the timeframe for evolution and development to a horizon counted not in thousands but in millions of years – the catching-up process, as well, might thus take much longer than anticipated. At the same time, race theorists cast doubt on the universal paradigm. Colonial societies, they claimed, might not just be late, but different altogether, without the possibility of ever matching the achievements of Europeans. In this situation, the trope of the Golden Age no longer only taught moral lessons, but also provided an identity to those that claimed to be the descendants of its inhabitants. The Golden Age was the proof of what they had been able to achieve in the past; it provided the answer to the question: "Who are we?" This identity transcended the dismal conditions visible in the present and brought in the past as proof of the community's potential: If they had done it once, they would be able to do it again, as the past was still present within them. The presence of a past of identity, both biological and historiographical, however, was different from the past the ghosts had brought to the present.

This argument allows us to bring in the emotional atmosphere, the *Stimmung*, accompanying this trope with more complexity than the usual equation of progress with pride and hope and of decline with shame and despair. The Golden Age did both: It held out a mirror in which the community could measure its decline from its former glory, but unlike the comparison with contemporary European powers, it also provided that community with the self-confidence that it would be strong enough to face the present and overcome it. These emotions neither canceled each other out nor did they simply add up. Rather, they created an intense blend that contained both hope and despair, but which could be subsumed under neither of them. This blend was more than an emotion: it created a *Stimmung* which suffused all other feelings.

The coloring and scent of the emotions, their *rang o bu*, reflected the varieties of the Golden Age depicted. Both Arabic and Urdu literature turned toward the time when Islam was not only victorious and dominant, but also leading in arts and sciences. A wealth of historical novels and epic poems focused on the early conquests, but even more on the Abbasid Empire, partly for its splendor but also as the center for the translation and adaptation of Greek philosophy and science (Hali, 1997; Perkins, 2011; Philipp, 2010). It was depicted as a model of an Islamic commonwealth not afraid of engaging with new knowledge, centered on a court that patronized philosophy, literature, and architecture, including gardens. Like these gardens, emotions and virtues too were cultivated and transformed into works of art. This model in no way contradicted the other Golden Age, the time when the Prophet himself led the first community of Muslims in Medina. As the Prophet was regarded as the most perfect of human beings and the seal of the prophets, after whom God would send no further revelation, this period had always been endowed with the highest religious authority and held out for emulation. What changed in the course of the twentieth century were the qualities of the Prophet and his companions that were emphasized and the emotional atmosphere this created. To an age striving for emotional balance and harmony had corresponded the wise statesman, who ended the age of ignorance, avoided every excess, and was mild and forgiving even toward his enemies. In the twentieth century, depictions increasingly showed the warrior, embodying manly valor, who had given up the softness of city life and rejoiced in the hardship of the battlefield, driven by relentless ardor and indomitable passion for the cause of God (Pernau, 2021).

For Indian Muslims, referring to an Islamic Golden Age was not without problems. Basing their identity on either Prophetic time or the Abbasid Empire certainly strengthened a pan-Islamic imaginary. However, the intellectual exchanges in which they participated were by no means limited to the colonial power and the Islamic world; they also involved debates, mutual influences, and cross-fertilization with different Hindu traditions, nearer in space and shared in daily interaction and practices. A Golden Age outside of India and based on religious belonging risked weakening those ties at a time when influential groups of Hindus, too, were opting for a Golden Age that foregrounded religious identity over territorial belonging. If the *satyayuga*, the age of truth, was too far back in time for a historical argument (it ended more than two million years ago), the Vedic time and its immediate aftermath were increasingly imagined as the ideal past, in which the Hindus were righteous, civilized, and powerful, before the Muslim and later the British conquests ended their cultural efflorescence (Chakrabarty, 1989; Kaviraj, 1995; Sarkar, 1998).

Not all Golden Ages in the Muslim world, however, emphasized Islam as the core identity holding the community and the nation together, even in countries where Muslims were in a majority. Since the second half of the nineteenth century, important voices in Iran had started to distance themselves from a common Islamic past. Mirza Fath-Ali Akhundzadeh (1812–78) and Mirza

Aqa Khan Kirmani (1854–97) propagated the image of an Iranian nation dating back at least 2,500 years, and finding its purest expression in the Golden Age before the advent of Islam. In increasingly racialized attacks, they depicted the invasion by the barbaric Arabs as the cause of decline. While these writings remained of limited influence during their authors' lifetime, they provided the basis for the official ideology under the Pahlavis (Zia-Ebrahimi, 2016). Much less influential and more short-lived was the Egyptian attempt to recreate the age of the Pharaohs as their national Golden Age in the 1920s (Wood, 1998).

The Golden Age was a highly mobile and adaptable global trope, which resonated widely and could be filled with various content by different people. One of the reasons that it worked so well in a plurality of contexts was that it could serve as a basis for very different strategies. At its most basic level, the knowledge that the community had known better, even glorious times in the past could lead to feelings of nostalgia, linking them back to Boabdil's last sigh. Nostalgia itself encompassed a variety of emotions of different intensity, ranging from a gentle mourning to anxious spasms of grief and the shedding of "tears of blood," as Urdu poets did not tire of describing (Pernau, 2015; Tignol, 2017). This form of nostalgia has been described as a passive emotion, characteristic of those who longed for the premodern age and refused to look or move forward, but also as sapping the energy needed for an eventual fight against modernity (Boym, 2001; Naqvi, 2007). Nostalgia is an emotion that invites in ghosts, especially in Urdu, where remembering puts the subject in a passive relation: "*mujhe yad ata hai*" ("memory comes to me"), instead of the English active voice ("I remember"). However, as the reference to the Iranian imagination of the pre-Islamic period has shown, the memory of a Golden Age and regret at its loss could also ally with much more dynamic and present-oriented emotions and practices. Here we find not only pride, but also feelings of vengeance and aggression directed against the group held responsible for ending the time of national preeminence. The past needs to be actively recalled and reinstated, but it also had never gone away, as, in their innermost core, the actors of the historical drama are the same in the present as they had been in the past: Race and biology, emphasizing the body, had started to take over the space once belonging to ghosts.

2.4 Renaissance

As mentioned in Section 2.3, the model of the stages of development, with its belief in a universal timeline sketched out by European history and geared toward linear progress, did not exclude the presence of other metaphors to make sense of the global diversity observed. Only in theory did the orientation of the stages of development toward the future and progress exclude the possibility of decline. In practice, it neither prevented the anxiety that European progress might not last forever nor negate the persistence of the older imagery, equating nations with living beings progressing through childhood, youth, middle age, toward senescence, and finally death. Progress in the first half of life did not discount decline in the second half. If Africa and other regions classified as not yet civilized were seen as child-like (and therefore in need of the fatherly guidance of the colonial powers), the Orient had outlived its civilizational blossom, becoming old and feeble (again, needing the colonial powers, in the prime of their lives, to take over). We will come back to this in more detail in Section 3.2.

However, European history also offered another set of images. Some authors viewed the Middle Ages as Europe's childhood, leading to the powerful manhood of the imperial age. But if the identification with Greek and Roman antiquity was not to be given up, they were also dark ages, following the decline of a powerful and highly cultivated empire, a period that could not be fitted into the metaphor of the life-cycle. The Renaissance provided a model for societies all over the world – from Ireland to Bengal and China – according to which a new life was possible, even after the Golden Age had been brought to an end (Mignolo, 1995; Mittler & Maissen, 2018; Schildgen, et al., 2006).

Reviving the past not only brought it into the present, the presence of the past in the present was also the only way to attain the future. However, such rebirth did not happen as a matter of course, nor did it happen for everyone. As the timeline was universal, there was no way out of medieval darkness except by passing through a renaissance. Remaining stuck in deathly darkness, however, was a very real possibility. It needed energy and courage to move along the timeline at a fast (or even a slow) pace, but also devotion and a willingness for sacrifice. The chance of a renaissance held out hope: If a society did reach this point, it offered the promise of a return to the Golden Age, perhaps even surpassing it. This was a hope that held a moral imperative, coloring that emotion in an activist hue. The activism, in turn, was only possible because the subjects of the present still carried within them the character and the emotions that had made the Golden Age possible, as a potential.

The semantics of the renaissance remain ambivalent. If the European Renaissance was called so only in the sixteenth century and found its enduring expression in the work of Jacob Burckhardt (1878 [1860]), the diverse renaissances of the Orient also used a variety of metaphors, from Hali's "ebb and flow" to the many images linked to sleep and awakening or to forgetfulness and remembrance. It is only from the end of the nineteenth century onward that the image of renaissance, of death and revival or rebirth, became dominant in the description of the movements in the recent past, and, in rare instances, also of those of the present.

The Bengal Renaissance was the first set of movements in nineteenth-century India to be called a renaissance, providing a blueprint for others. Its fascination with the Golden Age of Hinduism owed much to the endeavors of British Orientalists, who rediscovered and edited ancient Sanskrit texts (though it is not clear whether this knowledge had really been lost to the extent they claimed) (Chattopadhaya, 2002: 116, Tavakoli-Targhi, 2001). The Orientalists have traditionally been depicted in stark opposition to the Anglicists, who succeeded them and replaced their admiration for the Indian past with disdain and stopped the patronage for traditional learning in favor of English knowledge and literature. However, the authors of the Bengal Renaissance not only brought their temporal imagination into conversation with the British models, but were also willing to engage with English education and the tools they believed it provided them for overcoming the sleepiness of centuries and living up once again to the promise of the past. The presence of the past in their present provided them with the hope that a rebirth in the image of the past was possible. If this was to remain more than a nostalgic longing, exhortations exclaimed time and again, they had to become as active in their present as their forefathers had been in the Golden Age (Dasgupta, 2007; De, 1977; Hatcher, 2001).

The Nahda, the Arab Renaissance, resonated as a model for North Indian Muslims. As in the case of the Bengal Renaissance, the term was used for a diversity of movements stretching over several generations and bringing together a number of disparate goals. Napoleon's invasion of Egypt has often been mentioned as the triggering point. The top-down reforms of the military and the state administration under Muhammad Ali (1769–1849) were soon followed by an intellectual movement geared toward a revival of national and religious life (El-Ariss, 2018; Weiss & Hanssen, 2016; Zemmin 2018). Indian Muslims not only met the reformers during their travels to the Middle East, but also subscribed to their journals, notably to *al-Muqtataf* and *al-Manar*; at the end of the nineteenth century, the number of people able to read Persian and also some Arabic fluently was still high enough among the educated classes to allow for a relatively easy access. A detailed history of this engagement still needs to be written (for a path-breaking case study on Shibli Numani, see Bruce, 2016). For the few who had profound knowledge of Arab writers and their divergent positions, who took part in their debates and integrated them into their own writings, many more reacted emotionally to the fact that Muslims elsewhere, too, were awakening and shouldering the burden of reviving their lost heritage. After all, there are many things that can be done with a subscription to an Arab journal, from carefully reading it from cover to cover, to feeling pride in the presence of a material sign of the link to the heartland of Islam.

As these examples have shown, the renaissances neither developed independently of each other nor were they held together by a common program – not within any of the regions, and certainly not between them (moreover, not every region drew on the image of a renaissance – the Ottoman Empire's Turkish intellectuals seem to have sidelined this trope). What did, however, allow a resonance among renaissance proponents were the emotions associated with its image. The metaphor of a new life promised youth to the nation and a special role for the young. New life and youth, in turn, connoted heat, red bloodedness, and passion, as well as excitement, courage, and energy – all also associated with the virility of young men. Especially toward the end of the nineteenth century, the renaissance thus was not only perceived as an intellectual movement, but also involved bodies, first and foremost young male bodies, whose powerful potential had to be restored if the nation was to find new life (Balslev, 2019; Fischer-Tiné, 2001; Jacob, 2011). This topic will be taken up again in Section 3.3.

If the memory of the Golden Age still allowed ghosts to waft in and out of porous selves, if nostalgia could be experienced as a passive emotion, the shift within the semantic net from renaissance to awakening and arising (the more literal translation of *nahda*) shifted the agency from time and the past to individuals. The clarion calls "wake up!" and "arise!" resounded in the texts and speeches of the renaissances with an increasing urgency from the last third of the nineteenth century onward. The Darwinian revolution had lengthened the periods of history to an extent that made human agency seem irrelevant. Social Darwinism brought back hope, even if it was only the hope of battle and heroic sacrifice. Though renaissance and awakening were often used as synonyms, the discourse had reached a stage where the reference to the past seemed almost dispensable: The battle to raise a whole generation from the slumber of the ages could be directed toward a revival of the Golden Age, but it could also directly engage the future. Even more powerfully than the trope of the stages of development, the figure of the renaissance exorcised the ghosts. Or did it? While the goal was the strong sense of selfhood associated with manliness, the call to become men was not confined to the present, but also came from beyond – as did the help for their endeavors. "Mother, make me a man!" was the Hindu reformer Vivekananda's plea to the Goddess that resonated for an entire generation.

2.5 Reform

Especially in the colonial context, the nineteenth century has often been regarded as a century of reforms. This interpretation is not wrong, as in many countries the rise of European power exacerbated the need felt already earlier to take action to remedy the ills of the present. However, it has tended to obscure the longer history of reform movements, be it in precolonial North India or in the eighteenth-century Ottoman Empire. Reforms, in the original meaning of the word, aim at restoring a former and better state of affairs. As such, they need to assume some form of continuity through time. Only if human nature, the way the world works, and the values and rules for a virtuous life did not change with history, at least not fundamentally, could the restoration of the past be a viable program instead of an impossible anachronism.

According to Islamic belief, God leaves no community without guidance. Humanity, however, has an inherent tendency to move away from the revealed law, distorting the message and neglecting the commands. God periodically renewed the revelation until the sending down of the Quran to the Prophet Muhammad. Though the Quran was saved from corruption and has been preserved word for word as it was revealed, this did not change humankind's inclination towards decline. Therefore, each century, God sent a renewer of the faith, who recalled the believers to the original message and provided guidance for their reform. After the passing of the first millennium (calculated according to the Islamic calendar as starting from the migration of the Prophet to Medina, i.e., 1591 CE), a renewer of a special status would be sent. Shaikh Ahmad Sirhindi (1564–1624) was proclaimed to be this *mujaddid* (from *jadid*, "new"). He set out to guide the Muslims back to the purity of the revelation, eliminating accretions and innovations that, he argued, had crept in over time, not least through contact with people of other faiths and the misguided policy of the Mughal emperor Akbar to accommodate the interests of non-Muslims. Though his teachings were by no means undisputed, he had a lasting influence on the Islamic reform movement of the eighteenth century in India, as well as in Central Asia and in the Ottoman Empire, which emphasized the Quran and the Traditions of the Prophet as the only valid source of guidance (Buehler, 1998; Dahnhardt, 2002; Friedmann, 2000; Landau-Tasseron, 1989). The idea of a normative past to which a periodical return was needed as a condition for renewal did not remain limited to the religious sphere, but also provided arguments for reforms in the administration of the state, the "old law" (*kanun-i kadim*) taking the place of divine revelation (Topal, 2017).

Many of these movements started well before the colonial age. They fit neither into the narrative of Europe's awakening of the slumbering East, nor into the historical interpretation of the diffusion of reform ideas starting in the West and then adopted and adapted by the East. This is not to deny the importance of colonialism and its power structures in the nineteenth and twentieth centuries, but to point to the ongoing importance of precolonial tropes in the interpretation of the world under colonialism. *Islah*, reform aiming at restoration on condition of goodness or virtue as defined by the Holy Scriptures, remained a crucial concept throughout the nineteenth century and far into the twentieth. It provided a vital link between individual and social reforms. Once the rulers no longer guaranteed the Islamic character of the state – either because they lacked the necessary piety or because they had been displaced by a colonial government – this task fell to the individual believers. In the first instance, men from respectable families were called upon, but if they did not perform these duties, their wives and even the subalterns had to act on their own. Education, notably religious education focusing on the understanding of the Quran and the Traditions of the Prophet, was central to this endeavor. *Islah* was both a temporal concept, aiming at correcting behavior according to the historical model of the Prophet, and also the negation of history, as it referred to a revelation that brought God's unchanging eternity down into the world. It was reform, but it did not aim at introducing something new.

The second central concept – *tajdid* (also from *jadid*), reform as renewal of a previous state – was based on a more complex interplay of the old and the new. Not every past qualified as a normative reference for the present – least of all the past immediately preceding the present. Reform thus was new in comparison to what the past had become. In the same movement, however, the new reached back and linked up with the past of the Golden Age. Any movement toward the future was possible only through the presence, the appresentation, of this past through reform conceived as renewal in the image of the past.

Reform, in the shades of *islah* or *tajdid*, can evoke and be powered by a multiplicity of emotions. Especially in the North Indian case, research has focused on the displacement, since the nineteenth century, of what is considered an emotionally exuberant Islam open toward other religious communities and practices, grown out of interaction and accommodation, by a scripturalist, purist, and stern Islam, aiming at the discipline of emotions and keen to draw sharp boundaries. This opposition is often symbolized as a conflict between the Sufis and the Ulama, between the emotional mystic and the rigid scholar. This image is not completely wrong, though it is hard to draw a line between the Ulama and the Sufis, as most scholars were also initiated into mysticism, and many mystics were learned. Moreover, the emphasis on the Quran and the Traditions of the Prophet was no colonial import, of course, and reformist movements started well before British rule. Most importantly, it overlooks that reform, too, cultivated strong emotions. This could be a different love for the Prophet, turned into a bodily and daily habitus by the emulation of the minutest details of his comportment. This could also encompass the heavy burden of the responsibility for the salvation not only of one's own family, but of the entire community, which could no longer be delegated to the ruler or rely on the intercession of the dead-but-present saint. Once again, the banning of ghosts and jinns did little to alleviate fears and anxieties, but shifted them instead to different sites.

2.6 *Historia magistra vitae?*

Neither India nor the Islamic world were "a people without history," an unchanging "eternal Orient," whose inhabitants had neither interest in the past nor the ability to retrace it. However, the ways of perceiving the past and of establishing relations between the past and the present were numerous and could not be reduced to historiography. They encompassed a multiplicity of genres, some more factual while others were read as fictional by the audiences trained in detecting subtle cues to these differences (Rao, et al., 2003). The past was a storehouse of experience for the present and conveyed valuable lessons. History was indeed *magistra vitae*, the teacher of life. The past provided exempla for the moral law, bolstering it with experience. It showed the consequences of virtuous and vicious actions, held up heroes for admiration and emulation, and warned that ill-gotten gains of power and wealth were but temporary and would soon bring their retribution, as they always had. As the teacher of life, history both presupposed the continuity between the past, the present, and the future – only if the laws bringing about certain consequences did not change was it possible to learn from the past – and brought it about (Koselleck, 2004b). It was primarily those in a position to take decisions in the present – the rulers, the aristocracy, and the administration – who were to learn from the past. However, epics like the Shahnamah in Iran and the Mahabharata and Ramayana in India and, most importantly, religious history, the words and deeds of the Prophet and of saints, offered lessons for the common people and for the way they led their lives, even if they held no responsibility for the fate of state and society.

As argued earlier, this function of history never disappeared completely. If all experiences were devalued, if the laws of causality themselves were to change so quickly that cause and effect were to become random, no orientation would be possible. Regardless of whether causality existed or not, subjects would need to act as if it did, at least to some extent, if they wanted to act meaningfully at all and not remain "stranded in the present" (Fritzsche, 2004).

The disjunction – never complete, but also not to be neglected – between the space of experience and the horizon of expectation pointed toward an increasingly brittle relation between the past and the present. But this movement was nothing if not equivocal. History had by no means lost its importance since the beginning of the nineteenth century. Once the nation had been established as the new subject of history – a subject that moved through history, but was not subjected to change in its essential traits – a new continuity was created. The past now became "our" past; the nation mediated and guaranteed its presence in the present and in the future.

The past was seen as an objectively given reality that only needed to be discovered, but it was also perceived as a potential, a force for the revival and awakening of the nation. It was through knowledge of its past that the nation could recover its true identity. Bankimchandra Chatterjee, the Bengali novelist, caught this sentiment in a nutshell when he exclaimed in 1880, "Bengal must have a history, or else there is no hope for it." However, unlike the fluid, ghostlike past of previous times, this new past did not move into the present effortlessly; it needed the exertions of the subjects of the present. Bankim therefore continued: "Who will write it? You will write it. I will write it, all of us will write it. Every Bengali will have to write it" (quoted in Chatterjee, 1994: 4). To the degree that the past was no longer present, we can conclude, it was only as history and through history writing that it could be accessed. The ghosts had to be replaced by historiography, and this fundamentally altered the relation between the past and the present.

The buffered self and its corollary, the buffered present, which were no longer open to forces from the outside floating through them without invitation, certainly gained autonomy, or at least a feeling of autonomy. Whether the second part of the promise of the Enlightenment, the liberation from fear, had also been fulfilled can only be answered based on case studies. The mood Bankim evokes, his appeal to heroic action, but also the looming loss of hope, rather suggests that, at least in this case, one anxiety has been replaced by another, no less desperate. The past and the nation guaranteed each other, but the survival of the nation was by no means certain, unless the men (and later also the women) of the present sacrificed their all and themselves to save it.

Not all nationalism was based on this particular understanding of history. Early in his life, Gandhi explained that he had found truth not through the experience related by historical studies, but through experiments in his own life (Skaria, 2010). This implied a distance from the history of emperors in favor of the life of the villages, but went even further. If truth was unchanging, instead of being dependent on historical context, it was accessible – and for Gandhi, that always meant enactable – at every given moment. For Gandhi, the expression "the Kingdom of God is within you" (drawing on Tolstoi's interpretation of Luke 17:21) meant nothing less than the collapsing of the past, the present, and the future and the possibility to access eternity, truth, or God here and now. Ram Rajya, the rule of the king-god Ram, the protagonist of the epic Ramayana, took place neither in the past, nor would it happen in the future, after a long and arduous development. If people took the irrevocable decision to hold fast onto truth, not only the colonial rule, but even time and history would disappear and make place for independence, which only had meaning for Gandhi insofar as it embodied the kingdom of Ram, God, or Truth. On the one hand, this was the most extreme form of porosity between temporal categories imaginable, as it collapsed the very distinction between the past, the present, and the future, leaving room for neither nostalgia nor hope. On the other hand, whether this happened depended on the agency of the subjects: It was their decision to adhere to the truth, no matter what the cost, which could bring about complete independence and inaugurate the Golden Age.

3 The Presence of the Future

3.1 A Hauntology of the Future?

The past leaves traces in the present. Material objects remain for us to look at and to touch, texts – to read. Even if we do not always know how to read the information they convey about the past, we usually do not doubt that the past happened, that it cannot be changed any longer, and that it has an influence on the present. We may feel uncomfortable in bestowing a presence and an agency on the past (or recognizing it) once it is past, but we are confident that we can tell something, if not everything, about the past and link it to our present. If ghosts have an uncanny virtuality, which makes orthodox historiography doubt their existence, historians are real and know their job (or so we have to assume, if we want to continue reading and writing).

The future seems to work differently. Though the history of the future has taken off in recent years, it deals with what Koselleck called futures past: the imagination and knowledge of the future produced by historical subjects (2004a; see also Engerman, 2012; Graf, 2008; Hölscher, 2016; Radkau, 2017; Zaman, 2014). The future has not happened yet. Anticipations may not come true, and the unexpected is always possible. If the presence of the past in the present has an element of virtuality, this virtuality doubles up for the future: It is the virtual presence of something that has not even happened yet and might never happen at all, or so common sense tells us – things might become more complicated in the course of this section.

As we saw in the previous section, this common sense has evolved historically, and it was never as unequivocal as it might seem at first sight. In the Abrahamic religions, the time of the world was contained within eternal time. Eternity was the past of the world before creation and its future after the Last Judgment, but it also existed side by side with worldly time and could irrupt into it. The future, at least its broad outline, was known not through experience, but through revelation (Hölscher, 2016: 33). Within this outline, humans could shape their own future, always knowing that their acts would bring about their eternal destiny, unless God in his grace intervened.

Dreams were a classical point where God's grace and eternity touched the present, allowing individuals a glimpse into the future they were building for themselves. This opened up space for repentance and for a change of both the present and the future. Dreams in these traditions were believed to come not from a person's past, but to be caused by God, hence originating in a space beyond time and temporality. Examples in folktales and literature abound. In the Urdu context, the dream vision of the Day of Judgment that triggers the repentance and subsequent reform of Nasuh and his household in Nazir Ahmad's novel *Taubat un Nasuh* is probably the most famous one (2003 [1874]). Charles Dickens's *A Christmas Carol* forgoes the intervention of a personal god and transposes his agency onto ghosts, whose status remains vague. While the Ghosts of Christmas Past and Present had already shaken Scrooge's confidence, it is the appearance of the Ghost of Christmas Future that changes his life. Unlike the other ghosts, the shape of this presence remains hidden, showing only its eyes and a spectral hand. This does not make it any less real: It is the gaze *of* the future, "ghostly eyes intently fixed upon him" (Dickens 1920 [1843]: 122), even more than the gaze *into* the future that changes the present. It remains undecided whether "these [are] the shadows of the things that Will be or ... of the things that May be only" (149). But whatever the ontological status of the ghosts, their power to transform Scrooge is beyond doubt. What the encounter with the future changes most profoundly is Scrooge's emotions. No experience in the present could overcome his resistance to feeling anything toward his fellow human beings, but also toward the passing of time, and, in the end, toward himself. The gaze of the future not only evokes anxiety and even terror, but also the desperate need for hope and human relations. It is the promise that henceforth he will "live in the Past, Present and Future" that allows him to "sponge away the writing on this stone" (151).

The beliefs in ghosts and spirits coming from the future need more research to uncover their tremendous variety over space and time. This obviously cannot and need not be done here. What needs to be discussed, however, is how these religious beliefs and fictions can be made fruitful for a historical investigation. Neither religion nor literature can easily be translated into historical research. As discussed in the previous section, the agnostic standpoint of historiography often reaches its limit with the acknowledgment of the possible agency of ghosts, whether they come from the past or from the future. The secularism at the core of history writing as an academic discipline since the nineteenth century seems to demand that we recognize no other agency but that of presently living human subjects. Fighting off the porosity of the present, they are the only ones who can establish a relationship to the future, through their actions and their imaginations. The spectral presence of the future, looking at the present and transforming it, needed to be exorcised no less, or even more so, than the ghosts coming from the past, banishing it into the realm of privately held beliefs without relevance for the discipline.

In the twentieth century, the belief that everything depended on human agency not only informed historiography, but was widely shared on a global scale. Even for religious subjects, it seemed that God himself was asking them to act in the world as if everything depended on them and them alone: God helped those who help themselves, if he helped at all. Presence withdrew in favor of ethics. It could no longer be felt and it became doubtful whether it should be felt. Emotions had become a psychological phenomenon, not a way of knowing the world.

The more the openness of the future was emphasized, the more it became imperative to know the laws and rules that governed it. If this was not necessarily a contradiction, it at least created some tension. Unlike what Koselleck suggested, the horizon of expectation did not become vague once the future was deprived of the experience of the past, but gained precision through the exploration of historical laws. On the one hand, these laws governing the movement of history allowed the subjects to anticipate the consequences of their present actions on the future and thus foreclose possibilities, up to the point of Thatcher's infamous TINA – "There Is No Alternative" – which reduced the possibility of political decision to a right or wrong, best decided by technocrats. Future results thus played back on present options. On the other hand, this knowledge about the future made it possible to look at the present from the perspective of the future, to discover the future gazing at the present in a way reminiscent of the Ghost of Christmas Future. This future ghost or ghostly future was, its existence once again crossed out. Like an imagination, it lacked materiality, but it was also backed by the reality of the science of history and temporality. Every action in the present transformed the future, and only some of these transformations were reversible. Classifying these changes together with imaginations risked underestimating not only their importance, but also their material impact. The figure of future ghosts keeps alerting us to this in-between status: They are virtual, as the future has not happened yet, but the future which looks back at the present is not (only) an imagined one, it already has a reality which goes beyond imagination. Its effect on present subjects can equal posttraumatic stress in its intensity and reality. Indeed, pretraumatic stress disorder, first explored in fiction and films, is now starting to be considered a specific form of future-oriented anxiety (Kaplan, 2016; Saint-Amour, 2015).

Secularism was usually held to underwrite the openness of the future and human agency. With the same movement, however, future options foreclosed by present actions remained so for good, and could no longer be revised, no matter how sincere the repentance. Historians are only beginning to explore the emotions to which these developments gave rise. The assumption that the escape from the divine gaze unequivocally led to a feeling of liberation, relief, and pride in human agency might not be wrong, but rather insufficient to catch the complexity of the emotions. The gaze of the future, and the judgment coming generations would pass upon the present, might be as stern an admonition as any divine exhortation, perhaps even sterner, as they would no longer have the potential to forgive (and remedy) mistakes of the present generation. The possibility of creating the future, the increasing responsibility not only for one's individual life, but also for the fate of the community, of the nation, and even of the world, could be (and often was) exhilarating, but it might also weigh heavily. If the past provided an identity, it was under the gaze of the future – by acting responsibly not only for the present but also for future generations – that humans had to prove their character and their identities.

3.2 Decline, Degeneration, and Decadence

The trope of the stages of development was highly successful when it came to explaining how present differences evolved historically and how some European countries ended up at the spearhead of progress. It helped justify global hierarchy and inequality, while holding out hope that the so-called barbarous peoples were only not-yet civilized (Pernau, et al., 2015). The same trope was much less successful in predicting the future of these European countries. If progress was the law of history, it was possible to imagine it as unending, leading to an unlimited future. This future was yet unknown but for the fact that it would be even better and brighter than the present. Such an optimism, however, was challenged early on. The tropes of civilization and its critique were linked almost from the beginning. The very idea of civilizational progress, moral philosophers and political thinkers feared, might uncannily become its own undoing. The example of the Roman Empire, central for the Enlightenment, as well as for the Age of Revolutions, was used again and again to argue how a sense of security, urbanity, and refinement atrophied the very qualities that had brought about its grandeur. John Stuart Mill had warned already in 1836 that material, political, and cultural aspects of civilization might lead to the "relaxation of individual energy" (1905: 143). This would threaten the very foundation of the British Empire and everything it stood for, unless a reform of the educational system safeguarded the virtues, emotions, and bodies needed for its future survival, he argued.

As the nineteenth century progressed, these anxieties grew to an extent that they became central to the concept of modernity itself, or at least to its European experience. Progress had introduced the idea of movement into history, and this movement led to a constant acceleration, or so the contemporaries felt. The pace of life became quicker, epitomized by the railway, cutting through the landscape at increasing speed; work hours not only became longer, but the work also had to happen faster; rapid changes – factories and whole cities rising where a short time ago there had been pastures and villages – happened before one's eyes. By the turn of the century, this acceleration led to a medical and psychological discourse on neurasthenia, a mental illness triggered by an overstimulation of the nervous system, which affected an increasing number of patients across different walks of life, leaving them both overexcited and bereft of energy (Radkau, 1998). This was not happening at the margins, in the darkness of the colonies or their subaltern metropolitan counterparts, but at the heart of the countries that considered themselves the pinnacle of civilization. If progress, which implied further acceleration, was the inevitable law of history, the future would increasingly hold the danger of degeneration and decadence, unless strong measures were taken – or so an increasing number of Europeans feared at the turn of the century.

This had the potential to reconfigure the relations between the peoples thought civilized and those considered barbarous – who might now have more of a future than those doomed to progress, and hence decline. If European countries wanted to survive, the argument ran, they needed to forgo their emotional restraint and discipline, revert to the nature they had prided themselves on overcoming and once again become "red in tooth and claw." Contemporary experiences seemed to underwrite this interpretation, be it the French trauma of defeat in 1871, the British having to come to terms with the Boer war in 1902, the Russians with Japan's victory in 1905, or Germany with the debacle of the First World War and its aftermath. All of these experiences were read as warning signs. This gaze from the future onto the present transformed those experiences, vindicating earlier assumptions about the link between civilization and degeneration. The events were no longer read with reference to the present only, but conveyed an admonition from the future. It was the future itself that was in danger, even of being irrevocably lost, if no decisive action were taken, and taken immediately. Where barbarity was admired, it was not the barbarity of the colonized – racial prejudices would have prevented this – but of the colonial settlers, who lived in a dangerous environment no longer protected by civilization and who were a law onto themselves, which brought out the sterner qualities of a previous age, or so it was imagined.

It was only in theory that these emotions were incompatible with the ongoing pride in civilization. More than degeneration, decadence offered the possibility to assume the position of an observer, one who was not emotionally engaged in the outcome of the story, but watched it like a flâneur, observing with fascination the darkness, the abnormal, and the poisonous and transforming them into a work of art (Weir, 2018). Decadence marked the danger to civilization, but it could also be flaunted as a sign of civilization pushed to its very edge.

This story of acceleration, of nervous excitement, of fear of decline has often been read as a story of global modernity (Rosa, 2013). Lost battles, and, even more so, the fear of an extension of colonial rule to hitherto sovereign or semisovereign states, certainly were something that marked the history of the Muslim World in the nineteenth century, and increasingly so in the beginning of the twentieth. Much more than for Europe, decline here was not an anticipation of the future, but an experience of the present. The anxiety the future imparted was not so much about a further decline but about missing the chance for redemption, which might not reoccur in this lifetime or even longer than that.

We have too little empirical research to know precisely which of the European tropes and emotions resonated elsewhere and how they were linked to the traditional narratives of decline from a Golden Age, explored in the previous section. However, it seems that for many non-Western public figures, far longer and to a much greater extent than in Europe, modernity was not the illness of decline and degeneration, but its remedy and the possibility to overcome a downward trend originating in other causes. This held true for the interpretation of modernity as the age of science, one which would not only bring material benefits, but also overcome the superstition of the ages. Even at the sensory level, the experience of modernity might have been conspicuously different. The same railroads, telegraphs, factories, and new cities that Europeans linked to the overwhelming of the senses, and hence to modern diseases, brought forth distinctively different emotions when contrasted with the traditional sphere, often described in reformist literature and journals as the space of noise, foul smell, and chaos. Here, it was modernity that allowed for a feeling of peace and order. Degeneration was located in the cramped, lightless buildings of the old cities, which both colonial officers and local reformers linked to deficiencies at the level of the body no less than that of the character and the emotions.

The discourse on the future threatened by decline, degeneration, and decadence was closely linked to dangers to masculinity. Civilization might bring peace and safety from dangers, but it "unmanned the nation . . . emasculated the people and sapped their manhood" (Rai, 1917: 204). Nowhere does this become clearer than at the level of the emotions. *Jawanmardi*, the manliness of the young, has a long history in Iran and the Deccan, ruled by Shia kings in the late-medieval and early-modern periods (Balslev, 2019; Flatt, 2010). Young men, trained in various martial arts and especially in wrestling, represented an ideal masculinity not only in their bodies, but also in their emotions, notably in their courage and compassion, driving them to protect those less fortunate. Their masculinity translated into virility and energy (*himmat*), but also into red-blooded passions – here resonating with the traits desired by European prophets of degeneration, albeit coming from a different genealogy.

It was the denial of masculinity that constituted the utmost humiliation. This originated partly from a colonial discourse on the manly colonizer and the effeminate colonial subject (Chowdhury, 1998; Sinha, 1995) – the colonial denial of manliness struck deep even if there were other, local traditions the colonized might have tapped, such as medical knowledge of the Islamo-Greek tradition on the link between semen, blood, heat, and passion (Attewell, 2001, especially chapter 5; Gadelrab, 2011). Heat, in turn, was intimately linked to strong and redeeming passions (*josh*), courage, but also the fire of anger, which burned away impurities. In this, it was akin to the divine aspect of *jalal*, the terrifying majesty of God, linked to his honor, but also his justice. Female anger and implicitly also the anger of men lacking virility was deemed cold, and thus a despicable quality (Pernau, 2012).

It was in this manly *josh* that the hope for the future lay. Emotions were brought forth by the gaze toward the future and by the ghosts of the future staring back onto the present, but emotions were also central to the creation of a future. If only men felt strongly, they would still prevent their race from dying (Sanyasi, 1926), not only because their motivation would push them to action and sacrifice, but also because redemption, at both the individual and communal levels, lay in the emotions themselves, in their very intensity even before their actual content. Nevertheless, a number of emotions were central to arousing this fervor: anger against the oppressor; the heteroerotic love for the homeland, imagined as female (Najmabadi, 2005; Ramaswamy, 2010); the fraternal love among sons of the same mother; and compassion for all members of the community, including notably its weaker sections (Pernau, 2017).

Emotions, masculinity, and the modern subject they created, however, needed not only to be felt, but also to be seen and shown. This is the reason why in so many contexts, beards, mustachios (or their absence), clothes (notably trousers), and head coverings mattered to such an extent that they were enforced by law. In the twentieth century, in almost all Muslims countries, the long beard became the exclusive marker of the religious clergy; others were either clean-shaven (Turkey, Egypt), sported mustachios (Iran), or considerably shortened their beards, if not renouncing them altogether (India). The fez, introduced to the Ottoman Empire during the Tanzimat period, became a symbol of modernity and Pan-Islam, until Turkey banned it after the First World War and replaced it with the kepi, modeled after the French military uniform, while Iran chose the European civilian felt hat. In India, the choice of headgear followed politics – Congress-supporting Muslims wore a Gandhi cap, while others resorted to a variety of head coverings, or even none at all. Identities and allegiances were thus expressed by various markers. What they had in common was their demarcation from the past and the threat it held for the future; they not only symbolized a new masculinity, one that had overcome decline and degeneration, but also created it.

3.3 Utopia and the New Man

The call for the recovery of lost manhood fed into a larger program: the utopia of the creation of a new man, a new humanity, and a new world. This newness was no longer aimed at a recovery of the past, but reached out into a future that has never happened yet. It is true that already the cluster of tropes analyzed in the second section, all sharing the prefix re-, from renaissance to revival and restoration, was aimed at the future. But their future was conceived from the perspective of the past – the ghosts from the past were calling out to the present actors. It is precisely this perspective that became inverted in the tropes of utopia and the new man. Here, the ghosts from the future, the descendants who would live one day, and no longer the ancestors that had been, were those hailing the subjects of the present generation. The future would outshine the past and the present; far more than the present, it would be the space of a total newness. If Darwin's theory of evolution gave humanity a much longer past, extending even beyond the recognizable shape of humans, it also, with the same movement, extended the future: Evolution had not yet reached its goal, hence there was no knowing what humanity could still become. Nietzsche's fantasy of the overman also belongs here: "What is the ape to a human? A laughing stock or a painful embarrassment. And that is precisely what the human shall be to the overman: a laughing stock or a painful embarrassment" (2006 [1883]: 6). But evolution needed not only be conceived as biological – hopes for a new world, one of justice and virtue, and for new emotions were part of the same trope, which resonated across ideological boundaries.

Youth became a key category in this context. Education was central in creating a generation that was no longer held back by the burden of the past and could move forward; youth also continued to carry the association with *jawanmardi*, with hot blood and virile power. Most importantly, youth itself claimed a new role: The parents and the past were to be overcome, the young were the men (and a little later, also the women) of the future. This trope was highly mobile: If the generations of Young Germany, Young Italy, and Young Bengal had their heyday in the 1830s, Young Ireland followed about a decade later; the Young Ottomans were active from 1865 onward, the Young Turks and Young Arabs at the beginning of the twentieth century. The concept still held enough traction in 1918 for Gandhi to name his weekly journal *Young India*. This short overview already shows that, in most cases, the different movements did not share a common ideology beyond the trope itself. Transfers did happen in some cases; Young Italy was well known to the later Indian national movement (Bayly & Biagini, 2008), Young Bengal inspired Lajpat Rai in his book on Young India almost 80 years later (1917). But, once again, resonance did not need to be premised on detailed knowledge. What mattered was being part of a movement of the young rising and changing the world; what resonated was the images and emotions it evoked.

Across ideological boundaries, these movements shared a number of practices perhaps more aptly conceived as techniques of the future than as techniques of the self, or, more precisely, as techniques of creating the future with the aim of and premised on the creation of new selves. New Education was a pedagogical movement that aimed to overcome a way of teaching that focused exclusively on the development of the mind and intellect and the acquisition of knowledge. Instead, it placed the child and its faculties center-stage. The traditional emphasis on discipline and uniformity was to be replaced by the freedom to develop individuality; the acquisition of knowledge through books and the one-sided training of the rational faculty was to make way for a more holistic approach, providing children with a multitude of learning experiences and involving the body and the senses. From its European origins at the beginning of the twentieth century, New Education spread rapidly and became a global movement in the interwar period. Globally, it shared many practices for the creation of new men and women for a new world. The emphasis on work, manual and artisanal labor as well as gardening, and on art, dance, and theater created experiences that guided children to make their own discoveries and to learn to interpret them without imposing foregone conclusions. While the emotions addressing the future to be created through education were largely shared around the world, the feelings education aimed to bring forth in the children differed more widely. The German example, for instance, focused on education through a close and loving relation between teachers and pupils, which, in line with the concept of the pedagogical eros, could (and also did, in a number of cases) become eroticized and abusive. The Indian example, on the other hand, took up the emphasis the national movement of the late nineteenth century had already given to the overcoming of fear, thus embedding the pedagogy in a tradition reaching from Vivekananda to Gandhi and beyond (Keim & Schwerdt, 2013; Kumar & Oesterheld, 2007; Oelkers, 2005).

The global Scout movement, too, was geared toward training the young beyond traditional schooling, emphasizing the importance of outdoor education and the development of leadership skills. Unlike New Education, here the core aim was discipline of the body and of the mind, including the ability and willingness to be part of a hierarchy, to obey a leader, and in turn to expect obedience. This placed the scouts in many countries in the vicinity of paramilitary volunteer associations, which increasingly abounded in the interwar period (Balslev 2019; Honeck, 2018; Jacob, 2011; Roy, 2015; Watt, 2005). The military, but also a strictly organized work force, played a central role in the attempts of Nazi Germany, fascist Italy, and Stalin's Soviet Union to create new men (Dagnino, et al., 2017; Fritzsche & Hellbeck, 2008; Ponzio, 2015). Increasingly, these practices were underwritten by science, making use of psychology, notably behaviorism, in order to train people more effectively in the desired reactions, but also of medicine, hygiene, and eugenics, in order to breed new generations for the utopian future (Kashani-Sabet, 2000; Salgirli, 2011; Singleton, 2007).

Classical utopias, from Thomas Moore onward, were imaginations of an ideal society, described as situated in an unknown, perhaps even nonexisting place, but in parallel to the present time of the authors and their readers. The shift of utopias toward the future was a development of the eighteenth century. This responded in part to the constant shrinking of unknown spaces at a time when the Europeans were discovering the world, while also transforming their rationale from a critique of contemporary society to laying out what a future society would or at least might look like, and thus providing the goal to which present action should be directed. In the same movement, utopia lost its character as an imagination, always potentially plural and pluralistic, and was transformed into the one goal toward which the present was directed: The present might have emerged from the past, but both the past and the present lost their autonomy and existed only in reference to a single future (Koselleck, 2002).

If the new concept of pretraumatic stress disorder allows us to figure out how a future that has not happened yet is able to exert a presence in the present, utopia marks the other side: It anticipates not trauma, but salvation. In both cases, the present seems less important, but also less real than the ghosts that are coming from the future. The present is sacrificed for the future – most strongly in the totalitarian discourse and practices aiming at the new man, but also in the nationalist exhortation and the martyrdom it demanded from the present generation, with or without religious undertones. New Education could go either way: It recognized childhood and children as valuable in themselves, but it also worked under the ghostly gaze of the future and shared the dream of a new world.

These sacrifices evoked and required strong emotions. It is not by chance that the memories and histories of movements aiming at a utopian future abound with martyrs. The love for the motherland and for her children, the ardent desire to protect and liberate them, the importance of honor and shame have all been analyzed as part of the fight for the future, notably in the nationalist context. But emotions do more than motivate martyrs to die smilingly; emotions validate visions of the future and render them plausible to an extent beyond the reach of any rational argument. Emotions are both the goal and the means of creating new men and a new world. Learning to feel like a man (and, more rarely, like a woman) of the future, anticipating and practicing these future emotions until they form a habit and consolidate a character, shaping the mind and the body, and, finally, passing these on to the next generations were a duty that present subjects owed to the future, as authors and orators emphasized over and over again.

Still, one could argue that these futures did not really exist yet, that they were mere imaginations of the present. It was the present ventriloquizing as the future that had a presence, not the future, which has yet to happen. The relation between the present and the future, between existence and virtuality, might be more complicated than this. Utopias may have started out as imaginations (which, nevertheless, did not make them unreal in any uncomplicated way), yet these imaginations shaped not only the present, but also the future – which was probably much less open than we would usually like to assume. Once the present thus brought the future into existence, it lost its sole agency: The future now had a presence and it talked back, even if in a ghostly voice.

3.4 Revolution

Bringing about the utopian future takes time: a generation, if its medium is to be education; many generations, if it is to be based on the evolution of new bodies. Revolutions, on the contrary, are premised on a short-term transformation. The break with the past is instantaneous; the future is not on the distant horizon, but within immediate reach. Everything can change within a moment, once the existing powers are defeated. The clash between the old and the new is described in stark metaphors of darkness and light.

The first two decades of the twentieth century saw revolutions on a global scale (Motadel, 2021). The Russian revolution of 1905 was closely followed by the Iranian constitutional revolution, which ended the absolute power of the Qajar dynasty (Afary, 1996; Chehabi & Martin, 2010). The announcement of the partition of Bengal, also in 1905, led to the Swadeshi movement, a large popular mobilization aimed not only at a united Bengal, but also at a recovery of India from British colonialism. While the partition was revoked in 1911, the hoped-for radical transformation did not materialize. Radical revolutionaries – "terrorists," in colonial parlance – continued their work through underground organizations advocating violence (Ghosh, 2017; Sanyal, 2014). The next wave of revolutions came about at the end of the war, again starting with the Russian revolution of 1917, and continued with the Turkish revolt against the peace treaty of Sevres, which led to the war with Greece (1919–21) and internally to the end of the Sultanate in 1922 and the Caliphate two years later. Meanwhile, the Egyptian revolution against British occupation ended with formal Egyptian sovereignty, while still allowing ample influence to the colonial power.

This short overview already shows that not all revolutions lived up to the promise of radical change embedded in the temporality of the concept. The revolutions were a global phenomenon, each one providing both a model and the hope that change was indeed possible. Still, their reception was unequal – not only in the sense that Indian developments, as always, sparked less interest in the Middle East than the other way round. While the developments in the Arab countries were closely watched by Indian Muslims, events in Iran received less attention. The Ottoman Empire, on the other hand, had been a central reference point since the turn of the century. Notably, the Balkan wars led to a mobilization of the Indian Muslim public sphere. During the First World War, the defense of the Caliph was one of the central aims of the generation of young Indian Muslims, departing from the collaboration with the colonial government that had characterized the older generation, and instead striking an alliance with Gandhi and the Congress (Chatterji, 2013; Minault, 1982; Qureshi, 1999). In spite of a number of personal contacts and a continuous exchange of newspapers, the importance of Pan-Islam, centered on the person of the Caliph for Indian Muslims, blinded them to the changing perception of Islam and Islamic institutions in Turkey – the veneration of the Caliph and the admiration for the Turkish generals aiming to overthrow him went hand in hand. The abolition of the Caliphate took them completely by surprise and deprived them of their most important rallying symbol.

The most important influence on global revolutions was, of course, the Russian revolution of 1917. In India, it was taken up first not by the Bengali revolutionaries of Swadeshi origin, but by a movement that had started among

Punjabi migrants to the United States and was linked to their networks in Northwestern India. Reinterpreting the Uprising of 1857, commonly referred to as *ghadr*, as a revolution and as a forerunner of their own efforts, they combined anticolonialism with visions of social and economic transformations that opened up a utopian horizon, while also providing guidelines for the everyday struggle to attain it (Elam, 2014; Jan, 2018; Ramnath, 2011; Raza, 2020). Global revolutionaries from different countries became organized in international networks, coordinated by the Comintern and the Communist Party of the Soviet Union, which also provided support and training. Individual Muslims had taken part in the Ghadr movement from the beginning, some combining their previous Pan-Islamic worldview with communism (Ansari, 2014), while others left religious affiliation behind and fought for a future envisioned as rational and secular.

Revolutionary communism was probably more important in interwar India than was recognized by historiography until recently, dwarfed as it was by the Congress movement and the focus on the conflict between the Congress and the Muslim League, paving the way to the partition of the subcontinent. However, it was not party politics as much as literature that transformed social imagination and created a space for leftist politics. The Progressive Writers Movement was founded by Urdu-speaking students in London in 1935 under the leadership of Sajjad Zaheer and established in India in the following year. Promoting short stories, but also transforming poetic writing, it broached injustice, corruption, and hypocrisy, writing from the perspective of the socially marginalized and providing a canvas for the readers' empathy (Hunt, 2007). While they were abhorred by a large section of the public (the publication of their first collection of short stories leading to a prolonged court case targeting the way they dealt with sexuality), they remained one of the most influential literary movements for several decades. They opened the mental universe of a whole generation to ideas of revolution and of a future radically different from the present, thus creating the affective basis for new forms of orientation and alignment (Ahmed, 2009; Jalil, 2014).

Neither the imagination of a better future nor humanity's responsibility for bringing it about are exclusively modern developments. Religious traditions in particular provide rich visions: the new Jerusalem; the return of the Messiah; the *mujaddid* of the age, leading the community back to righteousness, power, and prosperity, to name only a few that were not necessarily otherworldly or deferred to the end of time. Humans knew what God asked them to do; their obedience or disobedience changed the course of history. The formulation of the stages of development secularized these imaginations and claimed to base them on science and the comparative study of history. Marx kept the basic outline of the model, but replaced the movement from savagery to civilization with one from slave societies to capitalism and extended it into the future by projecting the laws guiding the transition from one stage to the other onto the overcoming of capitalism by socialism and ultimately communism. The future in Marxism, but also in many of the other revolutionary movements, thus combined the certainty related to a scientific law with the duty to bring it about through revolutionary action.

As shown, before the First World War, the discourse on the decline and degeneration of the West had already had a strong impact on European countries, and perhaps even more so on their colonies, where the different national movements had increasingly combined a desire to acquire scientific knowledge from Europe with a refusal to adopt European culture. If they needed further proof that the aspired future was no longer to be found in the civilizational claims of Western countries, they found it in the carnage of the war, alongside the revolutions in many different regions of the globe. The future, it seemed to them, had already come about elsewhere, proving the validity of the laws of history and their predictive power – whether it was national liberation, the proclamation of a constitution enshrining civil rights and justice, or the communist revolution. It would only take time and struggle, which could not be anything but victorious, to bring about the same results in their own society. It was from these futures, the contemporary and the one to come, that the light illuminating the present shone and the voice resounded calling the present to be faithful to its duties. In the lives of the revolutionaries, the future was very much a presence that went beyond anything an individual or a collectivity could (or needed to) imagine.

This gave those movements emotional certitude. They not only knew what the future would bring, but, even more importantly, they were convinced that in the fight between the forces of the future and the past, they were on the right side. The feelings of shame, so striking in the words of nineteenth-century authors and orators, were no longer to be found. They might still have to fight, and they could not be sure whether the bright dawn would rise in their lifetime. But, whatever happened, they had no doubts about their ultimate victory. Even if in their eyes this certainty was based on science (and they would have scornfully brushed off any idea of ghosts), it did not lead to a cooling down of their emotional fervor. The proclaimed renunciation of the emotions was itself as passionate as could be: "We want people who may be prepared to fight without hope, without fear and without hesitation, and who may be willing to die un-honored, unwept and unsung," exclaimed Bhagat Singh. These fighters were to be found among the young, "because the young bear the most inhuman tortures smilingly and face death without hesitation. . . . The whole history of human progress is written with the blood of young men and women" (Habib, 2018: 30). The willingness to sacrifice one's own life and the legitimation to inflict violence went hand in hand and expressed the same emotions. The revolutionaries reached out impatiently for the future, spending no time thinking about the past and willing to forfeit the present, which was meaningful only insofar as it brought the future into being. If the love for the motherland still moved them, it was no longer the love for their ancestors, neither for the nation-mother or their siblings, but the love for the generations still to be born. Their identity was not bestowed on them by the past, by what they have been and still were potentially, but by the future, by what they may one day become. Again: These passions were not the other of discipline and obedience to rules, but their very fulfillment. It was only thus that Bhagat Singh could ask his fellow revolutionaries "to keep your cool, seeing your most beloved ones, whom you would like to keep before your eyes all the while, being sacrificed and tortured before you" (Habib, 2018: 6). The highest pitch of fervor was the sacrifice of the emotions themselves – this sacrifice, in turn, continued to fire the passions (Moffat, 2019).

3.5 Reform and Progress

The temporalities of the concept of reform are ambivalent. We have discussed reform as one of the tropes aimed at restoring a previous time, often imagined as a Golden Age, that provides an ongoing model for the present. As we have seen, this trope could be so powerful that it transformed the concept of progress. In the nineteenth century, *taraqqi*, though used as the standard translation for progress in Urdu, was not a concept of movement, geared toward an open future, but described a state that could be attained and, more importantly, had already been attained in the past. However, the concept of reform could also be used in a way that downplayed the restorative element of the word and provided an orientation not to the past, but to the future. This meaning gained importance throughout the nineteenth century, and by the turn of the century had absorbed the earlier connotations in most contexts.

This new concept of reform was closely tied to the expanding role of the state. Not only the European, but also the colonial state increasingly linked its own legitimation to initiating reforms, held to bring about civilization, progress, and, in the twentieth century, welfare. Almost from the moment that they became involved in the administration of India, colonial officers strove not only to understand the society and economy they wanted to govern, but also to reduce them to what they saw as rational principles. This applied to land revenue, attempting (not very successfully) to replace a system based on a multitude of overlapping entitlements to the produce of the soil with clearly defined rights, which were enforceable in court and which, they hoped, would incentivize an increase in productivity and hence also the share due to the state. This was also the impetus driving the reform of the legal system. Liberals such as Jeremy Bentham and the Governor General William Bentinck hoped that replacing despotism with the rule of law would transform a culture they claimed was based on fear, cowardice, and abject flattery and bring forth citizens capable of honesty and trust (Birla, 2009; Mantena, 2010). This went hand in hand with social reforms aimed at transforming the position of women – classically deemed one of the most important indicators for the civilizational stage of a society. The prohibition of Sati, the immolation of widows, was one of the most symbolic acts showing how white men saved brown women from brown men (Spivak, 1988). Other studies, however, have shown that this did not ameliorate the position of women, but, on the contrary, imposed the strict upper-caste regulations on an increasing number of groups (Chandra, 1998; Mani, 1999). Though laws related to family and marriage remained outside the purview of the state after the Revolt of 1857, this only slightly reduced the reforming drive of the British. Compared to European states of that time, the colonial state remained weak, but it certainly did not withdraw from its aim of governing and transforming society at any point in the nineteenth or twentieth centuries, increasingly acting in collaboration with Indian associations and, later, political parties (Khoja-Moolji, 2018).

Especially with reference to India, reforms by the state have often been analyzed within the framework of colonialism. This certainly makes sense, but a comparative angle might indicate that this is not the whole story. The history of the Ottoman Empire, Iran, and Egypt in the first half of the nineteenth century shows some similarities to the Indian development. Responding to an international situation that increasingly endangered their sovereignty, the rulers and their courts pushed for reforms to increase the power of the state and its access to resources. This meant, in the first place, a reforming of the army. The first engagements with Western knowledge were typically directed at the training of officers, familiarizing them with weapons, armaments, and military strategies currently used in the West, but also aiming to develop their potential to access this knowledge and then further it through training in the relevant languages, in mathematics, physics, and engineering, as well as in medicine. The desire to increase the military power of the state was also at the origin of many of the administrative reforms aimed at increasing the revenue of the state and the overall efficiency of the bureaucracy. In the end, the more effective management of resources required the state to mobilize the entire population in the reform movements – the expansion of the state through reforms happened no less under nationalism than under imperialism.

At first glance, these reforms do not seem to require a temporal imagination at all. They are directly responding either to a threat or to the felt need to expand the power of the state and the ruler. But a new concept of reform showed a changing orientation toward the future (Ringer, 2020). Whereas the traditional concepts of *islah* (rectification) and *tajdid* (renewal) had immobilized the concept of *taraqqi* (progress), it was now this concept that swallowed up the older meanings of reform and became a category of movement geared toward the future (Topal, 2017). Even if solutions were sought for present problems, in this new intellectual context actors believed they could only find them by overcoming the stasis of tradition and opening up toward the future, by accepting movement and permanent change as the basic condition of modernity. Politics that only took the present into consideration would not even protect the present. It was the gaze toward the future, its establishment at the core of the present, that guaranteed the salvation of both the present and the future. For men of power and privilege, this also meant averting the wrong, revolutionary future, but this was only one (if an important) aspect of the future they wanted to bring about.

However important the state had become for the enactment of reforms in the nineteenth century, and even more so in the twentieth, this does not imply that the role the public sphere, of associations, and of newspapers and journals had dwindled: Quite on the contrary, the reforming state and the public sphere advocating progress had become symbiotic. Journals became central in fleshing out the concepts of modernity and progress. It was here, notably in serialized travelogues and in articles describing the everyday life of the West, that the public could gather information on how modernity looked, how modern men and women behaved, and how it felt to be modern (Majchrowicz, 2015). Journals also provided the space to discuss reforms, pushing the state to be more active or warning about the dangers of a modernity that imitated the West – not to speak of lampooning those who adopted European dress and customs and got them all wrong (Ingram, et al., 2015).

Journals and associations were also an important venue for debates on women's reform, both in the sense of bettering women's lot in society and of improving their character and behavior. However, the debates on women's reforms and the reflections on the degeneration of the male body and the creation of new men worked quite differently. To a much greater extent than men, women were believed to symbolize their community and embody its honor, without being able to take an active role in its defense. Men not only defined how women had to be educated, how they had to behave and dress, they also took upon themselves to enforce these codes. Both the discourse on degeneration and loss of virility and the reform of women relied on shaming. But whereas the shaming of men was something they were able to actively counter through bodily practices and political action, women could avoid shame, or so the reformers told them, only by conforming to the agenda set up for them. Men could save themselves and redeem their honor; women had to wait to be saved. This logic worked across ideological divides, whether the veil was proclaimed as the sign of a pious woman, making visible the reformist piety of her family and her community, or whether forced unveiling marked her and the nation as modern. In both cases, female activity was not excluded, but was premised upon following the rules of men and the state.

The goal of progress, too, demanded an intense emotional mobilization. The fact that it became such a central object for the state and society eased the way to claiming the right to crush any opposition. Progress was held to produce new ways of feeling and being in the world: new ways of loving the spouse and the family, a new emotional engagement with the nation, and, not least, new longings to be satisfied by new commercial products. But progress was also an object of desire in itself, a passion for the future and the changes it promised – notably, for becoming a modern man or woman. The fact that these feelings were used to mobilize ever larger groups of people, by the state, but also by the economy – advertising has yet to be investigated as a major influence on conceptual change (Pernau, 2019c) – has often led to the suspicion that these emotions were only the result of manipulation, and hence a derivative phenomenon. To a certain extent, this is a valid observation, and strategies for creating emotions are certainly worth investigating. However, it is perhaps not helpful to assume intentionality – and hence an affective distance from the goals pursued – as the only explanation. If emotions, as discussed earlier, were what endowed temporalities and temporal concepts with plausibility, they were more often than not shared between those who aimed to propagate them and those who were to be taught how to be progressive, but also desired this instruction.

3.6 Development and Planning

Most of the tropes we have been looking at pertain to a global repertoire of temporal imagery available over a long time. This does not render them ahistorical, as the subjects selected them according to their requirements at each specific historical moment and adapted them to their needs. But in the same way that a trope like the Golden Age or the New Man can resonate across wide spaces, evoking emotions and creating communities without necessarily meaning the same thing everywhere, this was also possible across larger stretches of time. Some tropes look back to a long history, others developed only in the eighteenth and nineteenth centuries. What has interested us here is not so much when they were first created, but the moments in which they resonated with subjects, creating new communities of feeling and new ways of being in the world.

The tropes of development and planning follow a slightly different temporal logic. The history of planning goes back to the beginning of the twentieth century; it was implemented with the first five-year plan of the Soviet Union in 1928. Development became a new key concept after the Second World War, partly replacing civilization and linking up with planning as the most important practice for realizing its goals. Unlike for the earlier tropes, this happened almost simultaneously in most regions around the globe, and to a large extent also across ideological divisions: For several decades, the mastery of the future through planning, with the goal of developing society, economy, and the nation, was an understanding shared across the lines of the Cold War (Anderson, 2018; Hartmann & Vogel, 2010).

The proclamation of independence by an increasing number of former colonies brought about new ways of relating to time. For many decades, the national movements had devoted all their efforts to reaching this moment as their ultimate goal, the central event that would divide the present from the future. In this context, independence was more than the usual slow transformation of the future into the present. The future had begun now, and the new citizen-subjects were living it. For the first years, the present remained suffused by these former anticipations (which in the preceding years had already begun to include planning for the future after independence). But the present also came with a new future, and this future appealed to the present to develop the nation in order to fulfill earlier dreams about real independence. This did not exclude the awareness of history, but history – though important for identity and the question of "who are we?" – no longer provided models for the present. More even than the tropes of utopia and revolution on which it drew, development meant an interpellation from the future. As the Indonesian president Sukarno exclaimed in his opening speech at the Bandung conference: "I hope that it [the conference] will give evidence that Asia and Africa have been reborn, nay, that a New Asia and a New Africa have been born!" (*Asia-Africa Speaks from Bandung*, 1955: 28). The fact that these births took place in the present should not detract from the fact that the new nations would live toward the future and for the future.

If many tropes anticipating the future had been spread by intellectuals acting in the public sphere, often in opposition to the government of the day, development and planning were closely intertwined with state reforms and their desire for the enactment of modernity. The dream of leading their nations to economic development and thus transforming them into political powers on the international stage had brought together the leaders of the newly independent countries of Asia and Africa at Bandung. It allowed them to look at their own actions from a global vantage point and from an anticipated historical distance – humanity and the future would vindicate their actions, even if they had to push those they ruled beyond their present consent. The future – no longer the imagined future of utopia, but a scientifically proven and mathematically calculated one – was on their side (Chakrabarty, 2010; Lee, 2010; Shimazu, 2014).

For all the emotions of newness, the trope of development remained linked to its predecessor, civilization. It shared its universalism: the assumption that all nations and societies would have to pass through the same stages before reaching their ultimate goal. Unlike the earlier stages of development, the stages of economic growth, made famous by American economist Walt Whitman Rostow (1960), came with indicators that allowed the calculation of the present stage with mathematical precision. The scheme proclaimed five stages, marking the steps needed for the transition from traditional society to an age of high mass consumption – the ultimate goal. It also translated into an instruction manual, containing the measures to be taken to reach each next stage. Though Rostow and his theories need to be read in the context of the Cold War, being intended as a counter model to communist economic strategies, modernization remained a shared vision (Adalet, 2018; Cooper, 2010; Ekbladh, 2010; Latham, 2000; Macekura & Manela, 2018).

These models successfully combined two approaches to the future. On the one hand, modernization was nothing if not an ideology of permanent newness. If traditional society had been marked by its inertia and its resistance to change, modernization set history in motion, or so its proponents proclaimed, opening ever-new horizons and leading humanity into a future beyond what it might even imagine. On the other hand, the mathematical modelling of the stages of economic growth and futurology claimed that they have made the future predictable and even calculable. This was the basis for the practices of planning. Not only in the Soviet block and in India, with its Five Year Plans, but also in countries belonging to the Western alliance system, such as France, Germany, and Pakistan, planning had become the standard for any government activity (Gosewinkel, 2008; Van Laak, 2008). This involved setting economic goals and distributing resources. It also extended to urban development, the provision of housing, and the raising of new urban quarters or even cities – as important in war-destroyed Europe as in South Asia, where the Partition of 1947 led to millions of refugees, whom the government needed to resettle. Even in a field like education, planning was held to lead to an optimal allocation of funds ensuring a balanced development and the creation of the work force needed for the economic takeoff. Experts in the different areas of planning traveled widely, be it through development programs linked to specific donor nations, through the United Nations, or even as free consultants, who could be hired for specific tasks either by these organizations or by the governments. They contributed to the rapid diffusion of the new tools and the knowledge on which these were based; they were also important hinges, translating and linking the temporal imaginations of different groups (Adalet, 2018; Daechsel, 2015; Hartmann, 2020).

The universalism of the early economic models proved difficult to sustain once it became clear that the transition from underdevelopment to development did not happen as predicted. Studies on political culture aimed at introducing new variables, hoping to explain what went wrong and how measures needed to be modified to bring about the desired outcomes (Gabriel & Verba, 1963; Pye & Verba, 1965). Still, the euphoria of being able to plan for the future and to calculate the results of these actions marked the decades until the end of the 1960s.

At first glance, it would seem as if such a relation to the future would put an end to both emotions and ghosts. The way in which this engagement with the future was framed exalted science and rationalism. The past with its superstitions would be overcome, ghosts and the fears they evoked would be left behind, while humanity marched toward a better tomorrow, master of its own fate. What was needed to conquer the future were not the emotions of the poet, but the calculations of the engineer building the new dam and providing electricity to the countryside. But even this roughest of summaries shows that rationalism created its own pathos. No less than Sukarno's opening speech, Nehru's closing remarks at Bandung are a witness to the passions driving development: "We met because mighty forces are at work in these great continents, moving millions of people, creating a ferment in their minds, and urges and passions and a desire for a change from the present conditions." He and his allies from the newly independent countries of the world were "passionately eager to advance our countries peacefully. We have been backward; we are backward. We have been left behind in the race, in the world race and now we have got a chance again to make good. We want to make good and we have to make good rapidly because of the compulsion of events" (*Asia-Africa Speaks from Bandung*, 1955: 183–84).

The backwardness, once a cause for shame, became a starting point for limitless optimism, because the path into the future was clear – more than that, the future had already arrived. It would still take struggles and sacrifices, imparting a grave and even somber note to hope, and Nehru would have been the last to underrate the disturbances and dangers ahead and the need to mobilize all the resources for what he called the emotional integration of the country. But this did not call into question the faith and trust in the future.

This interpellation from the future was no longer negotiated through images of ghosts, at least not in the discourse which was hegemonic. This does not make their virtual presence in the present any less real. The Ghost of Future Christmas no longer presents Scrooge with a dreamlike vision of the future, but, like a development expert, shows him statistics and mathematical models and tells him how the looming disaster can be avoided: not through a moral conversion, or at least not foremost, but through planning. It was only when the global movements of 1968 started that this future of ever-increasing consumption for a constantly expanding strata of the population was called into question. The first oil crisis sent a warning that unlimited growth would not be sustainable.

4 Epilogue

With the previous section, we have almost reached our own time. In a final step, this epilogue will reflect on the challenges for the future of our planet, which are currently discussed under the label of the Anthropocene. In accordance with the overall topic of the Element, the emphasis will be neither on the causing factors of the Anthropocene nor on the political actions required, but on what it tells us about the currently shifting relations between the past, the present, and the future and the emotions undergirding these transformations.

The preceding pages have shown that the belief in the power of humans to shape the future, for better or worse, bringing about civilization and development or decadence and degeneration, is no invention of the twenty-first century. Especially monotheistic religions have long bestowed responsibility upon humanity; at an individual level, deciding about eternal salvation or damnation, but also collectively, from sin delaying the advent of the Messiah, leading God's people into exile, or resulting in lost wars or famines. This felt burden of responsibility did not diminish, but, indeed, grew with the loss in faith in a divine power, which could (and would) forgive humanity's faults and grant them a new beginning – an experience of loss that seemed more familiar to those brought up with a belief in karma. This responsibility and the emotions it evoked, however overwhelming they might have seemed to those experiencing them, remained limited to a certain extent. Negligence, a lack of commitment, or commitment for the wrong goals could seal the fate of a family, a community, or a nation for a couple of generations, but rarely touched the globe as a totality, and certainly did not bridge the boundary between humanity and nature. Whatever went wrong, the sun would still rise and set, and it would equally rain over the just and the unjust, the seasons would take their course, the rivers flow to the ocean, and the air be there for all living beings to breathe.

The reflections since the 1990s on whether a new era had started, one in which humanity has become a geological force (Ellis, 2018; Steffen, et al., 2007), changed this neat division between human history and natural history. Humanity, it was suggested, has become a geological force of its own, changing the course of planetary history and leaving traces that might remain for an unimaginably long time, possibly beyond the end of humanity as a species. This, in turn, meant that the timespans which needed to be taken under consideration extended not only much further into the past than even the evolutionary scale brought to attention by the Darwinian revolution, but also into a future that could no longer be measured by generations. Rather, the results of present policies on climate change might still be felt in 100,000 years or more, before they would be reversed by the next ice age (Stager, 2011) – some even talk about millions of years. Humans now straddled the history of the earth, the history of life on the planet, and the history since industrialization (Chakrabarty, 2009, 2021). Accordingly, there is not one future that needs to be taken into consideration, but a plurality of interconnecting futures, moving at different paces and hailing the present with different voices.

These futures are operating on very different time scales. They extend from climatic disruptions, which are already being felt in some regions of the earth and are expected to increase in the decades to come, to the extinction of many species and the profound transformation of what life on earth means, to the way the rising temperatures might prolong the interglacial phase by tens or hundreds of thousands of years. These changes were triggered in a short timespan – a little more than 200 years if the invention of the steam engine is taken as the starting point, 50 years when it is the increase in industrial production and consumption of fossil fuel since the 1950s. The time left to partially reverse these results is even shorter. These short times have to be brought into conversation and synchronized with the deep future impacted by these actions. But it also holds true the other way round: If impacts on the climate can be generated within a short time, our knowledge about developments not visible from the perspective of deep history – the disciplinary domain of historians – remains crucial. Migrations triggered by rising sea levels and desertification are not only an effect of climate change; they could lead to a political destabilization that might change the rules of politics within a couple of years, and hence also the possibilities for climatic actions, or even to violence at a scale that might have its own impact on the planet.

This changes the way we can think about the future: It is no longer unknowable, hidden behind a veil, and inaccessible. Political debates about the Anthropocene take up the tools already developed by futurology to predict and calculate the future. Computer modeling allows taking an increasing number of variables into consideration and investigating how, for instance, a rise in temperature of 1.5 degrees, as opposed to 3, will affect the sea level and aquatic life; or how certain forms of agriculture and livestock breeding will relate to the production of carbon dioxide and methane. These results, in turn, can form the basis for political debates.

These predictions are debated and constantly adapted as soon as new data comes in. However, there is an increasingly strong consensus that the Anthropocene is already with us. Even if everything was done immediately to stop its impact, the future of the earth, life, and the human species is no longer open, but marked by decisions taken in the past and the present. These consequences cannot be reversed, at least according to our present knowledge. We are constantly taking decisions, whether we are aware of it or not, that shape the present for future generations, for life on earth, and for the planet, creating a ghostly presence of the future. The ghosts of our descendants are coming to us from the future, haunting us and demanding justice, a justice that can only be obtained if times are viewed in synchronicity (Jordheim, 2017) and if we no longer shove the future into the great unknowable. The gazes from the present and from the future intersect. Political actions are possible only in the present, but they increasingly have to take the claims of the future into consideration; they operate within both the short term and the longue durée. In view of the impact we already had on the future, it is not possible to perceive these claims as mere present-day imaginations. Rather, they confront us with a reality from a different temporality: The present is becoming porous once again.

These changes in temporalities are affectively loaded. This poses a number of challenges to historians of emotions. The first, and perhaps the most obvious one, would be the development of a historical narrative leading up to the present. This could trace how the emotions linked to temporalities changed, perhaps from the hope for the future, fostered by faith in development and modernization in the 1950s (which, however, as we have seen, was never as unequivocal as it sometimes seems in hindsight), to present-day anxieties. However, emotions need to be traced in much greater detail before we can even attempt such a narrative. We need to look at the transformation of the category of anxiety, for instance, from a fin-de-siècle concern about degeneration of the race to present-day worries about the future of the planet. As historians of emotions, we would rightfully worry whether anxiety as a concept has a stable referent and if all different anxieties were experienced and felt in the same way (Dixon, 2020). Moreover, these emotions need no longer be analyzed as separate or even opposing feelings: the positive and future-affirming hope versus the dire warnings conveyed by anxiety. Rather, it might be more productive to investigate how these feelings mix, how a low-key worry, a mood rather than an emotion, is transformed into high-pitched anxiety, felt in the gut in events of natural and man-made catastrophes. Equally, mobilization through fear generates its own hope, different from the pride-infused hope based on the possibility of generating technological solutions for climate change.

At least as important as tracing changes from the past to the present is the reflection on the extent to which our circle of emotions has been limited by space and time, restricting our ability to feel solidarity, and how this might change in the future. The knowledge that we need to think and act in planetary categories and with the horizon of a deep future has hitherto seldom been underwritten by emotions. As we have seen in the preceding pages, the role of emotions is central in creating plausibility. However, as historians of emotions have shown convincingly, emotions are not a stable heritage coming to us from ancient times, but are shaped by our own cultural imaginations. What changes is not only the value we ascribe to them, but the very possibility to experience certain emotions (Frevert, 2011). Lynn Hunt has argued that the acceptance human rights gained in the eighteenth century was premised not least on the development of new ways of depicting the interiority of nonelite people through new techniques of narration in the novel (2007). Amitav Ghosh, in turn, has presented the case that it was up to present-day fiction writers to explore the imaginary of climate change (2016) and, we might add, to allow for the consideration of new emotions and affective temporal relations. Ghosh followed up these theoretical reflections in his novel *Gun Island* (2019), weaving together the depiction of climate change and migration with a Bengali folktale, figuring the conflict between the eponymous gun merchant, aiming to maximize his profits, and the goddess of snakes, Manasa Devi. Ghosh uses her figure to overcome long-settled dichotomies between the premodern and the modern, as well as between humans and other species, notably snakes and ghosts, without attempting to settle the question of the goddess's existence or nonexistence and her agency, neither for his audience nor even for the protagonists of the novel. This, in turn, allows him to avoid an easy holism – if only humans renounced modernity and became reconciled with the earth, everything would be well – and probe instead new ways of relating to the world, both cognitively and affectively.

The Anthropocene is most often talked and written about as a global phenomenon. Looking at development from the angle of human impact on the planetary history of the next hundreds of thousands of years, we certainly need this large perspective. However, it has also been pointed out that the actual experience of climate change is and will be increasingly different in various regions of the world. What has hardly been brought to the picture so far is the way in which these material changes are mediated locally, through cultural interpretations and emotions. To bring together the two central topics of Dipesh Chakrabarty's reflections, how can we provincialize the Anthropocene? How can we avoid it becoming, once again, a concept created and endowed with stable boundaries through European experiences, which is then applied to the rest of the world – where it fits, but not quite? We need local studies in a global perspective, geared toward the present, but anchored in a historical understanding, if we want to figure out how the changes of the Anthropocene lead to a transformation of the ways subjects situate themselves in time. Understanding emotions, their culturally specific formation, but also their global resonances, as this Element has hopefully shown, is central to this investigation.

Bibliography

Abu Lughod, Lila (1986). *Veiled Sentiments: Honor and Poetry in a Bedouin Society.* Berkeley: University of California Press.

Adalet, Begüm (2018). *Hotels and Highways: The Construction of Modernization Theory in Cold War Turkey.* Stanford: Stanford University Press.

Afary, Janet (1996). *The Iranian Constitutional Revolution, 1906–1911: Grassroots Democracy, Social Democracy, and the Origins of Feminism.* New York: Columbia University Press.

Ahmad, Nazir (2003 [1874]). *Taubat un Nasuh.* Lahore: Ferozsons.

Ahmed, Talat (2009). *Literature and Politics in the Age of Nationalism: The Progressive Writers' Movement in South Asia, 1932–56.* Delhi: Routledge.

Almond, Gabriel A. and Sidney Verba (1963). *The Civic Culture: Political Attitudes and Democracy in Five Nations.* Princeton: Princeton University Press.

Anderson, Jenny (2018). *The Future of the World: Futurology, Futurists and the Struggle for the Post-Cold War Imagination.* Oxford: Oxford University Press.

Ansari, Humayun (2014). Maulana Barkatullah Bhopali's Transnationalism: Pan-Islamism, Colonialism, and Radical Politics. In Götz Nordbruch and Umar Ryad, eds., *Transnational Islam in Interwar Europe: Muslim Activists and Thinkers.* New York: Palgrave Macmillan, pp. 181–209.

El-Ariss, Tarek, ed. (2018). *The Arab Renaissance: A Bilingual Anthology of the Nahda.* New York: The Modern Languages Association of America.

Asia-Africa Speaks from Bandung (1955). Jakarta: The Ministry of Foreign Affairs of the Republic of Indonesia.

Attewell, Guy Nicolas Anthony (2001). *Refiguring Unani Tibb: Plural Healing in Late Colonial India.* Hyderabad: Orient Longman.

Balslev, Sivan (2019). *Iranian Masculinities: Gender and Sexuality in Late Quajar and Early Pahlavi Iran.* Cambridge: Cambridge University Press.

Barak, On (2009). *On Time: Technology and Temporality in Modern Egypt.* Berkeley: University of California Press.

Barua, Rukmini, Alexandra Oberländer, Christa Hämmerle, and Claudia Kraft, eds. (forthcoming 2021). Fluid Feelings. Special issue, *L'Homme: Zeitschrift für feministische Geschichtswissenschaf* 32(2).

Baumann, Zygmunt (2000). *Liquid Modernity.* Cambridge: Polity Press.

Bayly C. A. and E. F. Biagini (2008). *Giuseppe Mazzini and the Globalization of Democratic Nationalism, 1830–1920*. Oxford: Oxford University Press.

Birla, Ritu (2009). *Stages of Capital: Law, Culture, and Market Governance in Late Colonial India*. Durham, NC: Duke University Press.

Böhme, Gernot (2017). *The Aesthetics of Atmospheres: Ambiances, Atmospheres and Sensory Experiences of Space*. London: Routledge.

Boym, Svetlana (2001). *The Future of Nostalgia*. New York: Basic Books.

Bruce, Gregory Maxwell (2016). Classical Islam Through Indian Eyes: The Many Histories of Shibli Nomani. PhD diss. The University of Texas at Austin.

Buehler, Arthur (1998). *Sufi Heirs of the Prophet: The Indian Naqshbandiyya and the Rise of the Mediating Sufi Shaykh*. Columbia: University of South Carolina Press.

Burckhardt, Jacob (1878 [1860]). *Civilization of the Renaissance in Italy*, trans. S. G. C. Middlemore. London: C. K. Paul & Co.

Chakrabarty, Dipesh (2001). *Provincializing Europe: Postcolonial Thought and Historical Difference*. Delhi: Oxford University Press.

Chakrabarty, Dipesh (2009). The Climate of History: Four Theses. *Critical Inquiry* 35, 197–222. https://doi.org/10.1086/596640.

Chakrabarty, Dipesh (2010). The Legacies of Bandung: Decolonization and the Politics of Culture. In Christopher J. Lee, ed., *Making a World after Empire: The Bandung Moment and Its Political Afterlives*. Athens: Ohio University Press, pp. 45–68.

Chakrabarty, Dipesh (2021). *The Climate of History in a Planetary Age*. Chicago: University of Chicago Press.

Chakrabarty, Uma (1989). Whatever Happened to the Vedic Dasi? Orientalism, Nationalism and a Script for the Past. In Kumkum Sangari and Sudesh Vaid, eds., *Recasting Women: Essays in Colonial History*. Delhi: Kali for Women, pp. 27–87.

Chandra, Sudhir (1998). *Enslaved Daughters: Colonialism, Law and Women's Rights*. Delhi: Oxford University Press.

Chateaubriand, François-René de (2006 [1821]). *Les aventures du dernier Abencerage*. Paris: Gallimard.

Chatterjee, Partha (1994). Claims on the Past: The Genealogy of Modern Historiography in Bengal. In David Arnold and David Hardiman, eds., *Subaltern Studies VIII: Essays in Honour of Ranajit Guha*. Delhi: Oxford University Press, pp. 1–49.

Chatterji, Rakhahari (2013). *Gandhi and the Ali Brothers: Biography of a Friendship*. Delhi: Sage Publishing.

Chattopadhaya, Utpal (2002). Indian Renaissance Reviewed. In Madhuri Santanam Sondhi, ed., *Hinduism's Human Face*. Delhi: Manak Publications, pp. 115–24.

Chehabi, H. E. and Vanessa Martin (2010). *Iran's Constitutional Revolution: Popular Politics, Cultural Transformations and Transnational Connections*. London: I. B. Tauris & Co.

Chowdhury, Indira (1998). *The Frail Hero and Virile History: Gender and the Politics of Culture in Colonial Bengal*. Delhi: Oxford University Press.

Civantos, Christina (2020). Writing on Al-Andalus in the Modern Islamic World. In Maribel Fierro, ed., *The Routledge Handbook of Muslim Iberia*. London: Routledge, pp. 598–619.

Clossey, Luke, Kyle Jackson, Brandon Marriott, Andrew Redden, and Karin Vélez (2016). The Unbelieved and Historians, Part I: A Challenge. *History Compass* 14, 594–602. https://doi.org/10.1111/hic3.12360.

Cooper, Frederick (2010). Writing the History of Development. *Journal of Modern European History* 8(1), 5–23. http://www.jstor.org/stable/26265901.

Daechsel, Markus (2015). *Islamabad and the Politics of International Development in Pakistan*. Cambridge: Cambridge University Press.

Dagnino, Jorge, Matthew Feldman, and Paul Stocker (2017). *The "New Man" in Radical Right Ideology and Practice, 1919–45*. London: Bloomington.

Dahnhardt, Thomas (2002). *Change and Continuity in Indian Sufism: A Naqshbandi-mujaddidi Branch in the Hindu Environment*. Delhi: D. K. Printworld.

Dasgupta, Subrata (2007). *The Bengal Renaissance: Identity and Creativity from Rammohun Roy to Rabindranath Tagore*. Delhi: Permanent Black.

Davis, Erin Calhoun (2009). Situating "FLUIDITY": (Trans) Gender Identification and the Regulation of Gender Diversity. *GLQ* 15(1), 97–130. https://doi.org/10.1215/10642684-2008-020.

De, Barun (1977). A Historiographical Critique of Renaissance Analogues for Nineteenth Century India. In Barun De, ed., *Perspectives in Social Sciences I*. Calcutta: Oxford University Press, pp. 178–218.

Derrida, Jacques (2006). *Specters of Marx: The State of the Debt, the Work of Mourning and the New International*, trans. Peggy Kamuf. New York: Routledge.

Dickens, Charles (1920 [1843]). *A Christmas Carol in Prose: Being a Ghost Story of Christmas*. Boston: Little, Brown and Company.

Dixon, Thomas (2020). What is the History of Anger a History of? *Emotions: History, Culture, Society* 4(1), 1–34. https://doi.org/10.1163/2208522X-02010074.

Eisenlohr, Patrick (2018). *Sounding Islam: Voice, Media, and Sonic Atmospheres in an Indian Ocean World*. Berkeley: University of California Press.

Ekbladh, David (2010). *The Great American Mission: Modernization and the Construction of an American World Order*. Princeton: Princeton University Press.

Eksell, Kerstin (2011). The Legend of Al-Andalus: A Trajectory across Generic Borders. In Kerstin Eksell and Stephan Guth, eds., *Borders and Beyond: Crossings and Transitions in Modern Arabic Literature*. Wiesbaden: Harrassowitz, pp. 103–26.

Ekshakry, Marwa (2013). *Reading Darwin in Arabic, 1860–1950*. Chicago: University of Chicago Press.

Elam, J. Daniel (2014). Echoes of Ghadr: Lala Har Dayal and the Time of Anticolonialism. *Comparative Studies of South Asia, Africa and the Middle East* 34(1), 9–23. https://doi.org/10.1215/1089201X-2648551.

Ellis, Erle (2018). *Anthropocene: A Very Short Introduction*. Oxford: Oxford University Press.

Engerman, David C. (2012). Introduction: Histories of the Future and the Futures of History. *The American Historical Review* 117(5), 1402–10. www.jstor.org/stable/23426552.

Ernst, Carl (2016). *Refractions of Islam in India: Situating Sufism and Yoga*. Delhi: Sage Publications.

Faruqi, Shamsur Rahman (1995). Constructing a Literary History, a Canon, and a Theory of Poetry: *Ab-e Hayat* (1880) by Muhammad Husain Azad. *Social Scientist* 23, 269–71.

Felek, Ozgen and Alexander D. Knysh, eds. (2012). *Dreams and Visions in Islamic Societies*. New York: Suny Press.

Fischer-Tiné, Harald (2001). "Character Building and Manly Games": Viktorianische Konzepte von Männlichkeit und ihre Aneignung im frühen Hindu Nationalismus. *Historische Anthropologie* 9(3), 432–55. https://doi.org/10.7788/ha.2001.9.3.432.

Flatt, Emma (2010). Young Manliness: Ethical Culture in the Gymnasiums of the Medieval Deccan. In Anand Pandian and Daud Ali, eds., *Ethical Life in South Asia*. Bloomington: Indiana University Press, pp. 153–73.

Frevert, Ute (2011). *Emotions in History: Lost and Found*. Budapest: Central European University Press.

Friedmann, Yohanan (2000). *Shaykh Ahmad Sirhindi: An Outline of His Thought and a Study of His Image in the Eyes of Posterity*. Delhi: Oxford University Press.

Fritzsche, Peter (2004). *Stranded in the Present: Modern Time and the Melancholy of History*. Cambridge: Harvard University Press.

Fritzsche, Peter and Jochen Hellbeck (2008). The New Man in Stalinist Russia and Nazi Germany. In Michael Geyer and Sheila Fitzpatrick, eds., *Beyond Totalitarianism: Stalinism and Nazism Compared*. Cambridge: Cambridge University Press, pp. 302–42.

Frumer, Yulia (2018). *Making Time: Astronomical Time Measurement in Tokugawa Japan*. Chicago: University of Chicago Press.

Gadelrab, Sherry Sayed (2011). Discourses on Sex Differences in Medieval Scholarly Islamic Thought. *Journal of the History of Medicine and Allied Sciences* 66(1), 40–81. https://doi.org/10.1093/jhmas/jrq012.

Gammerl, Benno, Philipp Nielsen, and Margrit Pernau, eds. (2019). *Encounters with Emotions: Negotiating Cultural Differences since Early Modernity*. New York: Berghahn.

Ghosh, Amitav (2016). *The Great Derangement: Climate Change and the Unthinkable*. Chicago: University of Chicago Press.

Ghosh, Amitav (2019). *Gun Island*. New York: Farrar, Straus and Giroux.

Ghosh, Durba (2017). *Gentlemanly Terrorists*. Cambridge: Cambridge University Press.

Ghosh, Ranjan and Ethan Kleinberg, eds. (2013). *Presence: Philosophy, History and Cultural Theory for the Twenty-First Century*. Ithaca, NY: Cornell University Press.

González-Reimann, Luis (2016). Cosmic Cycles, Cosmology, and Cosmography. In Knut A. Jacobsen, Helene Basu, Angelika Malinar, and Vasudha Narayanan, eds., *Brill's Encyclopedia of Hinduism Online*. Leiden: Brill.

Gosewinkel, Dieter (2008). Zwischen Diktatur und Demokratie: Wirtschaftliches Planungsdenken in Deutschland und Frankreich: Vom Ersten Weltkrieg bis zur Mitte der 1970er Jahre. *Geschichte und Gesellschaft: Zeitschrift für historische Sozialwissenschaft* 34(3), 327–59. https://doi.org/10.13109/gege.2008.34.3.327.

Graf, Rüdiger (2008). *Die Zukunft der Weimarer Republik*. Munich: R. Oldenbourg Verlag.

Granara, William (2005). Nostalgia, Arab Nationalism, and the Andalusian Chronotope in the Evolution of the Modern Arabic Novel. *Journal of Arabic Literature* 36(1), 57–73. https://www.jstor.org/stable/4183530.

Gumbrecht, Hans Ulrich (2004). *The Production of Presence: What Meaning Cannot Convey*. Stanford, CA: Stanford University Press.

Habib, Irfan, ed. (2018). *Inqilab: Bhagat Singh on Religion and Revolution*. Delhi: Yoda Press.

Hali, Altaf Husain (1997). *Hali's Musaddas: The Flow and Ebb of Islam*, trans. Javed Majeed, ed. Christopher Shackle. Delhi: Oxford University Press.

Har Dayal, L. (1934). *Hints for Self-Culture*. London: Watts & Co.

Hartmann, Heinrich (2020). *Eigensinnige Musterschüler: Ländliche Entwicklung und internationales Expertenwissen in der Türkei (1947–1980)*. Frankfurt: Campus.

Hartmann, Heinrich and Jakob Vogel, eds. (2010). *Zukunftswissen: Prognosen in Wirtschaft, Politik und Gesellschaft seit 1900*. Frankfurt: Campus.

Hartog, François (2015 [French original 2003]). *Regimes of Historicity: Presentism and Experiences of Time*, trans. Saskia Brown. New York: Columbia University Press.

Hatcher, Brian A. (2001). Great Men Waking: Paradigms in the Historiography of the Bengal Renaissance. In Sekhar Bandyopadhyay, ed., *Bengal: Rethinking History, Essays in Historiography*. Delhi: Manohar, pp. 135–66.

Hermansen, Marcia (2005). *The Conclusive Argument from God: Shah Wali Alla of Delhi's Hujjat Allah al-Baligha*. Delhi: Kitab Bhavan.

Hirschkind, Charles (2020). *The Feeling of History: Islam, Romanticism, and Andalusia*. Chicago: University of Chicago Press.

Hoffmann, Stefan Ludwig and Sean Franzel (2018). Introduction: Translating Koselleck. In Reinhart Koselleck, *Sediments of Time: On Possible Histories*, trans. and ed. Stefan-Ludwig Hoffmann and Sean Franzl. Stanford, CA: Stanford University Press, pp. ix–xxi.

Hölscher, Lucian (2016). *Die Entdeckung der Zukunft*. Göttingen: Wallstein.

Honeck, Mischa (2018). *Our Frontier is the World: The Boy Scouts in the Age of American Ascendancy*. Ithaca, NY: Cornell University Press.

Hunt, Lynn (2007). *Inventing Human Rights: A History*. New York: W.W. Norton.

Huyssen, Andreas (2003). *Present Pasts: Urban Palimpsests and the Politics of Memory*. Stanford, CA: Stanford University Press 2003.

Ibn Khaldun (1958). *The Muqaddimah: An Introduction to History*. New York: Pantheon Books.

Ingram, Brannon D., J. Barton Scott, and SherAli Tareen, eds. (2015). Imagining the Public in Modern South Asia. Special issue, *South Asia: Journal of South Asian Studies* 38(3).

Irving, Washington (2017a [1832]). *Tales of the Alhambra*. N.p.: Musaicum Books.

Irving, Washington (2017b [1828]). *Chronicle of the Conquest of Granada*. N. p.: Musaicum Books.

Jacob, Wilson Chacko (2011). *Working Out Egypt: Efendi Masculinity and Subject Formation in Colonial Modernity, 1870–1940*. Durham, NC: Duke University Press.

Jalil, Rakhshanda (2014). *Liking Progress, Loving Change: A Literary History of the Progressive Writers' Movement in Urdu*. Delhi: Oxford University Press.

Jan, Ammar Ali (2018). In the Shadow of Ghadar: Marxism and Anti-Colonialism in Colonial Punjab. *Socialist Studies/Études socialistes* 13(2), 58–80. https://doi.org/10.18740/ss27202.

Jordheim, Helge (2011). Does Conceptual History Really Need a Theory of Historical Times? *Contributions to the History of Concepts* 6(2), 21–41. https://doi.org/10.3167/choc.2011.060202.

Jordheim, Helge (2017). Synchronizing the World: Synchronizing as Historical Practice, Then and Now. *History of the Present* 7(1), 59–95. https://doi.org /10.5406/historypresent.7.1.0059.

Joshi, Priya (2002). *In Another Country: Colonialism, Culture and the English Novel in India*. New York: Columbia University Press.

Kaplan, Ann E. (2016). *Climate Trauma: Forseeing the Future in Dystopian Film and Fiction*. New Brunswick: Rutgers University Press.

Kashani-Sabet, Firoozeh (2000). Hallmarks of Humanism: Hygiene and Love of Homeland in Qajar Iran. *The American Historical Review* 105(4), 1171–203. https://doi.org/10.2307/2651407.

Kaviraj, Sudipta (1995). *The Unhappy Consciousness: Bankimchandra Chattopadhyay and the Formation of Nationalist Discourse in India*. Bombay: Oxford University Press.

Keim, Wolfgang and Ulrich Schwerdt (2013). *Handbuch der Reformpädagogik in Deutschland (1890–1933). Teil 1: Gesellschaftliche Kontexte, Leitideen und Diskurse*. Frankfurt: Peter Lang GmbH, Internationaler Verlag der Wissenschaften.

Khan, Saiyid Ahmad (1962). Junun ki haqiqat. In M. I. Panipati, ed., *Maqalat-e Sir Saiyid*. Vol. II. Lahore: Majlis-e taraqqi-e adab, pp. 135–83.

Khoja-Moolji, Shenila (2018). *Forging the Ideal Educated Girl: The Production of Desirable Subjects in Muslim South Asia*. Oakland, CA: University of California Press.

Kleinberg, Ethan (2017). *Haunting History: For a Deconstructive Approach to the Past*. Stanford, CA: Stanford University Press.

Koselleck, Reinhart (2000). Einleitung. In Reinhart Koselleck and Hans-Georg Gadamer, *Zeitschichten: Studien zur Historik*. Frankfurt: Suhrkamp, pp. 9–16.

Koselleck, Reinhart (2002). *The Practice of Conceptual History: Timing History, Spacing Concepts*, trans. Todd Presner, Kerstin Behnke, and Jobst Welge. Stanford: Stanford University Press.

Koselleck, Reinhart (2004a). *Futures Past: On the Semantics of Historical Time*, trans. Keith Tribe. New York: Columbia University Press.

Koselleck, Reinhart (2004b). Historia Magistra Vitae: The Dissolution of the Topos into the Perspective of a Modernized Historical Process. In *Futures Past: On the Semantics of Historical Time*, trans. Keith Tribe. New York: Columbia University Press, pp. 26–42.

Koselleck, Reinhart (2004c). "Space of Experience" and "Horizon of Expectation": Two Historical Categories. In *Futures Past: On the Semantics of Historical Time*, trans. Keith Tribe. New York: Columbia University Press, pp. 255–75.

Koselleck, Reinhart (2011). Introduction and Prefaces to the *Geschichtliche Grundbegriffe* (Basic Concepts in History: A Historical Dictionary of Political and Social Language in Germany), trans. and ed. Michaela Richter. *Contributions to the History of Concepts* 6(1), 1–37. https://doi.org/10.3167/choc.2011.060102.

Koselleck, Reinhart (2018). Structures of Repetition in Language and History. In Reinhart Koselleck, *Sediments of Time: On Possible Histories*, trans. and ed. Stefan-Ludwig Hoffmann and Sean Franzl. Stanford: Stanford University Press, pp.158–74.

Koselleck, Reinhart (2020). Fiery Streams of Lava, Frozen into Memory. Many Farewells to War: Memories which are Not Interchangeable, trans. Margrit Pernau and Sébastien Tremblay. *Contributions to the History of Concepts* 15(2), 1–6. https://doi.org/10.3167/choc.2020.150201.

Koselleck, Reinhart and Hans-Georg Gadamer (2000). *Zeitschichten: Studien zur Historik*. Frankfurt: Suhrkamp.

Kumar, Krishna and Joachim Oesterheld (2007). *Education and Social Change in South Asia*. Hyderabad: Orient Longman.

Landau-Tasseron, Ella (1989). The "Cyclical Reform": A Study of the *Mujaddid* Tradition. *Studia Islamica* 70, 79–117. https://doi.org/10.2307/1595679.

Landwehr, Achim (2016). *Die anwesende Abwesenheit der Vergangenheit: Essay zur Geschichtstheorie*. Frankfurt: S. Fischer.

Langewiesche, Dieter (2021). Historische Anthropologie und Sprache bei Reinhart Koselleck: Geschichtliche Prognostik als Wiederkehr der *Historia Magistra Vitae*? In Manfred Hettling and Wolfgang Schieder, eds., *Reinhart Koselleck als Historiker: Zu den Bedingungen möglicher Geschichten*. Göttingen: Vandenhoeck & Ruprecht, pp. 425–38.

Latham, Michael E. (2000). *Modernization as Ideology: American Social Science and "Nation Building" in the Kennedy Era*. Chapel Hill, NC: The University of North Carolina Press.

Lee, Christopher (2010). *Making a World after Empire: The Bandung Moment and Its Political Afterlives*. Athens: Ohio University Press.

Leys, Ruth (2000). *Trauma: A Genealogy*. Chicago: University of Chicago Press.

Lorenz, Chris (forthcoming [2021]). Probing the Limits of Metaphor. On the Stratigraphic Model in History and Geology. In Zoltán Boldizsár Simon and Lars Deile, eds., *Historical Understanding: Past, Present and Future*. London: Bloomsbury.

Lorenz, Chris, Berber Bevernage, and Aleida Assmann, eds. (2013). *Breaking up Time: Negotiating the Borders between Present, Past and Future*. Göttingen: Vandenhoeck & Ruprecht.

Lutz, Catherine (1988). *Unnatural Emotions: Everyday Sentiments on a Micronesian Atoll and Their Challenge to Western Theory*. Chicago: University of Chicago Press.

Lytton, Edward Bulwer (1838). *Leila or the Siege of Granada*. London: Longman, Orme, Brown, Green and Longmans.

Macekura, Stephen J. and Erez Manela, eds. (2018). *The Development Century: A Global History*. Cambridge: Cambridge University Press.

Majchrowicz, Daniel (2015). Travel and the Means to Victory: Urdu Travel Writing and Aspiration in Islamicate South Asia. PhD diss., Harvard University.

Mani, Lata (1999). *Contentious Traditions: The Debate on Sati in Colonial India*. Delhi: Oxford University Press.

Mantena, Karuna (2010). *Alibis of Empire: Henry Maine and the Ends of Liberal Imperialism*. Princeton: Princeton University Press.

Masarwah, Nader and Abdallah Tarabieh (2014). Longing for Granada in Medieval Arabic and Hebrew Poetry. *Al-Masaq: Journal of the Medieval Mediterranean* 26(3), 299–318. https://doi.org/10.1080/09503110.2014.969068.

Mignolo, Walter D. (1995). *The Darker Side of the Renaissance: Literacy, Territoriality, & Colonization*. Ann Arbor, Michigan: University of Michigan Press.

Mill, John Stuart (1905 [1836]). Civilization. In *The Works of John Stuart Mill. IV: Dissertations and Discussions*. London : G. Routledge & Sons; New York: E.P. Dutton & Co., pp. 130–67.

Minault, Gail (1982). *The Khilafat Movement: Religious Symbolism and Political Mobilization in India*. New York: Columbia University Press.

Mittermaier, Amira (2011). *Dreams That Matter: Egyptian Landscapes of the Imagination*. Berkeley: University of California Press.

Mittler, Barbara and Thomas Maissen (2018). *Why China Did Not Have a Renaissance and Why that Matters: An Interdisciplinary Dialogue*. Berlin: Walter de Gruyter.

Moffat, Chris (2019). *India's Revolutionary Inheritance: Politics and the Promise of Bhagat Singh*. Cambridge: Cambridge University Press.

Molina, Luis (2020). The Integration of Al-Andalus in Islamic Historiography: The View from the Maghrib and the Mashriq. In Maribel Fierro, ed., *The Routledge Handbook of Muslim Iberia*. London: Routledge, pp. 572–85.

Motadel, David (2021). Global Revolution. In David Motadel, ed., *Revolutionary World: Global Upheaval in the Modern Age*. Cambridge: Cambridge University Press, pp. 1–37.

Najmabadi, Afsaneh (2005). *Women with Mustaches and Men without Beards: Gender and Sexual Anxieties of Iranian Modernity*. Berkeley: University of California Press.

Naqvi, Nauman (2007). The Nostalgic Subject: A Genealogy of the "Critique of Nostalgia." *Cirsdig Working Paper* 23, 2–55.

Nietzsche, Friedrich (2006 [1883–85]). *Thus Spoke Zarathustra: A Book for All and None*, ed. Adrian Del Caro and Robert B. Pippin, trans. Adrian Del Caro. Cambridge: Cambridge University Press.

Noorani, Yaseen (1999). The Lost Garden of Al-Andalus: Islamic Spain and the Poetic Inversion of Colonialism. *International Journal of Middle East Studies* 31, 237–54. https://www.jstor.org/stable/176294.

Nünlist, Tobias (2015). *Dämonenglaube im Islam: Eine Untersuchung unter besonderer Berücksichtigung schriftlicher Quellen aus der vormodernen Zeit (600–1500)*. Boston, MA: De Gruyter.

Oelkers, Jürgen (2005). *Reformpädagogik: Eine kritische Dogmengeschichte*. Weinheim: Juventa.

Ogle, Vanessa (2015). *The Global Transformation of Time: 1870–1950*. Cambridge: Harvard University Press.

Perkins, Christopher Ryan (2011). Partitioning History: The Creation of an *Islami Pablik* in Late Colonial India, c. 1880–1920. PhD diss., University of Pennsylvania.

Pernau, Margrit (2012), Male Anger and Female Malice: Emotions in Indo-Muslim Advice Literature. *History Compass* 10(2), 119–28. https://doi.org/10.1111/j.1478-0542.2012.00829.x.

Pernau, Margrit (2013). *Ashraf into Middle Classes: Muslims in Nineteenth Century Delhi*. Delhi: Oxford University Press.

Pernau, Margrit (2015). Nostalgia: Tears of Blood for a Lost World. *South Asia Graduate Research Journal (SAGAR)* 23, 74–109.

Pernau, Margrit (2016). Provincializing Concepts: The Language of Transnational History. *Comparative Studies of South Asia, Africa and the Middle East* 36(3), 483–99. https://doi.org/10.1215/1089201x-3699031.

Pernau, Margrit (2017). Love and Compassion for the Community: Emotions and Practices among North Indian Muslims, c. 1870–1930. *The Indian*

Economic and Social History Review 54(1), 21–42. https://doi.org/10.1177 /0019464616683480.

Pernau, Margrit (2019a). *Emotions and Modernity in Colonial India: From Balance to Fervor.* Delhi: Oxford University Press.

Pernau, Margrit (2019b). Fluid Temporalities: Saiyid Ahmad Khan and the Concept of Modernity. *History and Theory* 58(4), 107–31. https://doi.org/10 .1111/hith.12138.

Pernau, Margrit (2019c). Modern Masculinity, Bought at Your Local Pharmacist: The Tonic Sanatogen in 20th-century Indian Advertisements. *Tasveer Ghar: A Digital Archive of South Asian Popular Visual Culture.* www.tasveergharindia.net/essay/sanatogen-masculine-advert.html.

Pernau, Margrit (2021). The Time of the Prophet and the Future of the Community: Temporalities in Nineteenth and Twentieth Century Muslim India. *Time & Society.* https://doi.org/10.1177/0961463X20987720.

Pernau, Margrit, Helge Jordheim, Orit Bashkin, et al. (2015). *Civilizing Emotions: Concepts in Nineteenth-Century Asia and Europe.* Oxford: Oxford University Press.

Pernau, Margrit and Max Stille (2021). Obedient Passion – Passionate Obedience: Ashraf Ali Thanawi's Sermons on the Love of the Prophet. *Journal of Religious History* 45, 25–49. https://doi.org/10.1111/1467-9809 .12727.

Philipp, Thomas (2010). *Jurji Zaidan and the Foundations of Arab Nationalism.* Syracuse, NY: Syracuse University Press.

Ponzio, Alessio (2015). *Shaping the New Man: Youth Training Regimes in Fascist Italy and Nazi Germany.* Madison: The University of Wisconsin Press.

Pye, Lucian W. and Sidney Verba (1965). *Political Culture and Political Development.* Princeton: Princeton University Press.

Qureshi, M. Naeem (1999). *Pan-Islam in British Indian Politics: A Study of the Khilafat Movement, 1918–1924.* Leiden/Boston: Brill.

Radkau, Joachim (1998). *Das Zeitalter der Nervosität: Deutschland zwischen Bismarck und Hitler.* Munich: Carl Hanser Verlag.

Radkau, Joachim (2017). *Geschichte der Zukunft: Prognosen, Visionen, Irrungen in Deutschland von 1945 bis heute.* Munich: Carl Hanser Verlag.

Rai, Lajpat (1917). *Young India.* New York: B. W. Huebsch.

Ramaswamy, Sumathi (2010). *The Goddess and the Nation: Mapping Mother India.* Durham, NC: Duke University Press.

Ramnath, Maia (2011). *Haj to Utopia: How the Ghadar Movement Chartered Global Radicalism and Attempted to Overthrow the British Empire.* Berkeley: University of California Press.

Rao, Velcheru Narayana, David Shulman, and Sanjay Subrahmanyam (2003). *Textures of Time: Writing History in South India, 1600–1800*. New York: Other Press.

Raza, Ali (2020). *Revolutionary Pasts: Communist Internationalism in Colonial India*. Cambridge: Cambridge University Press.

Ringer, Monica M. (2020). *Islamic Modernism and the Re-Enchantment of the Sacred in the Age of History*. Edinburgh: Edinburgh University Press.

Rosa, Hartmut (2013). *Social Acceleration: A New Theory of Modernity*, trans. Jonathan Trejo-Mathys. New York: Columbia University Press.

Rosa, Hartmut (2019). *Resonance: A Sociology of our Relationship to the World*. Hoboken: Wiley.

Rostow, Walt Whitman (1960). *The Stages of Economic Growth: A Non-Communist Manifesto*. Cambridge: Cambridge University Press.

Roy, Franziska (2015). International Utopia and National Discipline: Youth and Volunteer Movements in Interwar South Asia. In Ali Raza, Franziska Roy, and Benjamin Zachariah, eds., *The International Movement: South Asia, Worlds and World Views, 1917–39*. Delhi: Sage, pp. 150–87.

Runia, Eelco (2014). *Moved by the Past: Discontinuity and Historical Mutation*. New York: Columbia University Press.

Rushdie, Salman (1995). *The Moor's Last Sigh*. London: Penguin.

Saint-Amour, Paul K. (2015). *Tense Future: Modernism, Total War, Encyclopedic Form*. Oxford: Oxford University Press.

Salgirli, Sanem Güvenç (2011). Eugenics for the Doctors: Medicine and Social Control in 1930s Turkey. *Journal of the History of Medicine & Allied Sciences* 66(3), 281–312. https://doi.org/10.1093/jhmas/jrq040.

Sanyal, Shukla (2014). *Revolutionary Pamphlets, Propaganda and Political Culture in Colonial Bengal*. Delhi: Cambridge University Press.

Sanyasi, Shraddhanand (1926). *Hindu Sangathan: Saviour of the Dying Race*. Delhi: Arsh Sahitya Prachar Trust.

Sariyannis, Marinos (2019). *A History of Ottoman Political Thought up to the Early Nineteenth Century*. Leiden: Brill

Sarkar, Sumit (1998). Renaissance and Kaliyuga: Time, Myth and History in Colonial Bengal. In Sumit Sarkar, *Writing Social History*. Oxford: Oxford University Press, pp. 186–216.

Schildgen, Brenda Deen, Gang Zhou, and Sander L. Gilman, eds. (2006). *Other Renaissances: A New Approach to World Literature*. New York: Palgrave Macmillan.

Sharar, Abdul Halim (1899). *Flora Florinda*. Delhi: Qaumi Press.

Shimazu, Naoko (2014). Diplomacy as Theatre: Staging the Bandung Conference of 1955. *Modern Asian Studies* 48(1), 225–52. https://doi.org/10.1017/S0026749X13000371.

Simon, Zoltán Boldizsár (2019). *History in Times of Unprecedented Change: A Theory for the 21st Century.* London: Bloomsbury.

Singleton, Mark (2007). Yoga, Eugenics, and Spiritual Darwinism in the Early Twentieth Century. *International Journal of Hindu Studies* 11(2), 125–46. www.jstor.org/stable/25691059.

Sinha, Mrinalini (1995). *Colonial Masculinity: The "Manly Englishman" and the "Effeminate Bengali" in the late 19th Century.* Manchester: Manchester University Press.

Skaria, Ajay (2010). The Strange Violence of Satyagraha: Gandhi, Ithiass, and History. In Manu Bhagavan, ed., *Heterotopias: Nationalism and the Possibility of History in South Asia.* Delhi: Oxford University Press, pp. 142–85.

Spivak, Gayatri (1988). Can the Subaltern Speak? Speculations on Widow Sacrifice. In Cary Nelson and Lawrence Grossberg, eds., *Marxism and the Interpretation of Culture.* Chicago: University of Illinois Press, pp. 271–313.

Stager, Curt (2011). *Deep Future: The Next 100,000 Years of Life on Earth.* New York: Thomas Dunne Books.

Steffen, Will, Paul J. Crutzen, and John R. McNeill (2007). The Anthropocene: Are Humans Now Overwhelming the Great Forces of Nature? *Ambio: A Journal of the Human Environment* 36(8), 614–21. https://www.jstor.org/stable/25547826.

Syros, Vasileios (2012). An Early Modern South Asian Thinker on the Rise and Decline of Empires: Shāh Walī Allāh of Delhi, the Mughals, and the Byzantines. *Journal of World History* 23(4), 793–840. https://www.jstor.org/stable/41858765.

Taneja, Anand Vivek (2018). *Jinnealogy: Time, Islam, and Ecological Thought in the Medieval Ruins of Delhi.* Stanford, CA: Stanford University Press.

Tareen, SherAli K. (2019). *Defending Muhammad in Modernity.* Notre Dame, IN: University of Notre Dame Press.

Tavakoli-Targhi, Mohamad (2001). *Refashioning Iran: Orientalism, Occidentalism and Historiography.* Hampshire, NY: Palgrave Macmillan.

Taylor, Charles (2007). *A Secular Age.* Cambridge, MA: Belknap Press of Harvard University Press.

Tignol, Eve (2017). Nostalgia and the City: Urdu *Shahr Ashob* Poetry in the Aftermath of 1857. *Journal of the Royal Asiatic Society* 27(4), 559–73. https://doi.org/10.1017/S135618631700013X.

Topal, Alp Eren (2017). From Decline to Progress: Ottoman Concepts of Reform 1600–1876. PhD diss., Ihsan Dogramaci Bilkent University.

Van Laak, Dirk (2008). Planung: Geschichte Und Gegenwart Des Vorgriffs Auf Die Zukunft (Planning: The Past and Presence of Advancing the Future). *Geschichte Und Gesellschaft* 34(3), 305–26. www.jstor.org/stable/40186216.

Watt, Carey Anthony (2005). *Serving the Nation: Cultures of Service, Association, and Citizenship*. Delhi: Oxford University Press.

Weir, David (2018). *Decadence: A Very Short Introduction*. Oxford: Oxford University Press.

Weiss, Max and Jens Hanssen, eds. (2016). *Arabic Thought beyond the Liberal Age: Towards an Intellectual History of the Nahda*. Cambridge: Cambridge University Press.

Wellbery, David E. (2010). Stimmung. In Karlheinz Barck, Martin Fontius, Friedrich Wolfzettel, and Burkhart Steinwachs, eds., *Ästhetische Grundbegriffe: Historisches Wörterbuch in sieben Bänden*, Vol. 5. Stuttgart: Metzler, pp. 703–33.

Wishnitzer, Avner (2015). *Reading Clocks, Alla Turca: Time and Society in the Late Ottoman Empire*. Chicago: University of Chicago Press.

Wood, Michael (1998). The Use of the Pharaonic Past in Modern Egyptian Nationalism. *Journal of the American Research Center in Egypt* 35, 179–96.

Zaidan, Jurji (2010 [1903]). *The Conquest of Andalusia*, trans. Roger Allen. Bethesda, MD: Zaidan Foundation.

El-Zain, Amira (2009). *Islam, Arabs and the Intelligent World of the Jinn*. Syracuse, NY: Syracuse University Press.

Zaman, Faridah (2014). Futurity and the Political Thought of North Indian Muslims, c. 1900–1925. PhD diss., University of Cambridge.

Zemmin, Florian (2018). *Modernity in Islamic Tradition. The Concept of "Society" in the journal al-Manar (Cairo, 1898–1949)*. Berlin/Boston: Walter de Gruyter.

Zia-Ebrahimi, Reza (2016). *The Emergence of Iranian Nationalism: Race and the Politics of Dislocation*. New York: Columbia University Press.

Acknowledgments

Most of the research and all of the reading for this Element have been done in my pandemic home office. Anja Berkes, with her usual efficiency, nevertheless found ways to keep me supplied with an unending stream of books. Alp Eren Topal, my go-to person for everything Ottoman and beyond, patiently answered all my questions. Florian Zemmin did the same for the Arab world and carefully read the entire manuscript. Without their help, I would never have ventured beyond my North Indian comfort zone.

Frederik Schröer, Luc Wodzicki, Daniel Kolland, and Sébastien Tremblay have been my partners in crime for all things temporal for many years. They, as well as Ben Miller, also read several sections of this text. They have challenged my interpretations and fought with my ghosts, but also encouraged me to pursue the project.

Over the years, successive generations at the Center for the History of Emotions at the Max Planck Institute for Human Development have shaped my thinking on emotions. Rukmini Barua, Steffi Lämmert, Alex Oberländer, and Esra Sarioglu have brought my attention to the concept of fluidity in gender studies and queer theory, and I have thoroughly enjoyed our discussions and our common project on gender and fluidity. Niv Savariego has been the perfect assistant and copy editor.

Jan Plamper has been the best of friends and editors, both demanding and encouraging, and giving me the space to explore my ideas. The two anonymous reviewers read the text with care and goodwill and helped me clarify my meaning at important points.

Several audiences of South Asianists encouraged me to welcome ghosts into my research. Martin Fuchs, Rajeev Bhargava, and Neeladri Bhattacharya at the International Center for Advanced Studies, Metamorphoses of the Political, Delhi; Kama MacLean and Ute Hüsken at the South Asia Institute in Heidelberg; Laurence Gautier at Jindal University; and Faisal Devji, David Lelyveld, and Rosalind O'Hanlon at Oxford deserve special mention.

A huge thank you to all of them; I could not have done it without you, and I hope that we will continue our conversation.

Cambridge Elements ☰

Histories of Emotions and the Senses

Jan Plamper
University of Limerick

Jan Plamper is Professor of History at the University of Limerick. His publications include *The History of Emotions: An Introduction* (Oxford, 2015); a multidisciplinary volume on fear; and articles on the sensory history of the Russian Revolution and on the history of soldiers' fears in World War One. He has also authored *The Stalin Cult: A Study in the Alchemy of Power* (Yale, 2012) and *Das neue Wir: Warum Migration dazugehört. Eine andere Geschichte der Deutschen* (S. Fischer, 2019).

About the Series
Born of the emotional and sensory "turns," Elements in Histories of Emotions and the Senses move one of the fastest-growing interdisciplinary fields forward. The series is aimed at scholars across the humanities, social sciences, and life sciences, embracing insights from a diverse range of disciplines, from neuroscience to art history and economics. Chronologically and regionally broad, encompassing global, transnational, and deep history, it concerns such topics as affect theory, intersensoriality, embodiment, human-animal relations, and distributed cognition.

Cambridge Elements ⹀

Histories of Emotions and the Senses

Printed in the United States
by Baker & Taylor Publisher Services

Printed in the United States
by Baker & Taylor Publisher Services